AS-Level History

Pursuing Life and Liberty: Equality in the USA (1945-68)

There's a lot to learn if you're studying AS-Level History.

Luckily, this book takes you through everything you need to know for Unit 1, Option D5, with plenty of analysis to help you see why things happened the way they did. Plus, it's got loads of practice questions to test your knowledge.

It also has a whole section on how to turn what you've learnt into a top-notch exam answer, to help you prepare for the big day.

And of course, we've done our best to make the whole thing vaguely entertaining for you.

Complete Revision and Practice

Exam Board: Edexcel (Unit 1, Option D5)

Published by CGP

Editors:
David Broadbent, Luke von Kotze

Contributors:
Peter Callaghan, Vanessa Musgrove

Proofreaders:
Claire Boulter, Hugh Mascetti

Acknowledgements

With thanks to Rex Features for permission to use the images on pages 8, 10, 12, 16, 23 & 26
With thanks to Getty Images for permission to use the images on pages 32 & 38

ISBN: 978 1 84762 673 8

Groovy Website: www.cgpbooks.co.uk

Printed by Elanders Ltd, Newcastle upon Tyne.

Based on the classic CGP style created by Richard Parsons.

Contents

Introduction to the Unit

Section 1 — The Civil Rights Movement, 1945-1955

Section 2 — King and Peaceful Protest, 1955-1968

Section 3 — Malcolm X and Black Power

Section 4 — Ethnic Minorities' and Women's Rights

Section 5 — Exam Skills

Section 6 — Writing Your Answer

Background to the USA

America has a pretty interesting history, and some of it will be useful for you to know when you do this topic. But don't learn everything about America, like its favourite colour, or where it'd like to go on a romantic date. It's just not helpful...

The **Population** of the **US** is formed of **Different Ethnic Groups**

1) **Native Americans** — are the **indigenous** people of America. Their **population fell rapidly** from the **15th century** due to **war** with, and **diseases** brought by, **European colonists**.
2) **Europeans** — From the **15th century**, **colonists** from **Britain**, **France** and **Spain explored** and **settled** in America.
3) **Africans** — In the **17th century**, colonial powers **bought slaves** from **Africa** to America. These slaves often **worked** on the **land** or as **household servants** and were an **important part** of **America's economy**.
4) **Mexicans** — Much of the **southwest** of what is now the **US** belonged to **Mexico** until **1848**. Many **Mexicans** who **lived** there **stayed**, and **millions** more would later **emigrate** to the **US**. **Mexico** was a **Spanish colony** until **1821** and its **inhabitants** were **descendants** of **Native Americans** and **Spanish settlers** — they were **ethnically different** to **white Americans**.

America was a **Nation Divided**

1) In **1861** civil war broke out in America. It was fought between the **Union states** (known as the **North**) and the **states** of the **Confederacy** (the **South**).
2) One of the main causes of the war was the **South's** decision to **secede** (become a separate country) in order to keep the system of **slavery**. Slavery had been a vital part of its **economy** for **over 200 years**.
3) In **1865** the **Confederacy** was **defeated**, and the United States of America was **reunited** under a **single government** in **Washington, D.C.** Congress then agreed the **13th Amendment**, which **abolished slavery**.

Things seemed to be **Getting Better** for **African Americans**

1) After the **Civil War** there was a period known as **Reconstruction**, where the **US reunited politically**, **socially** and **economically**. The US government tried to **force** the **South** to give **former slaves** their **rights**.
2) During Reconstruction **several changes** were made to the **US Constitution** (see p.3) to provide **legal rights** for **former slaves**. By **1870 black men** could **vote** and **hold public office** — e.g. become **judges** or **members** of **Congress**. It seemed that the **prospects** of **African Americans** were **improving**.
3) **However**, white **Southerners united** to **resist** the **legal changes**, often using **violence** and **intimidation**.

The Confederate states are regarded as being the 'Southern' states. Some other states also had segregation, such as Oklahoma and Kentucky.

> The **Ku Klux Klan** was formed **after** the **Civil War**. Its aim was to **maintain** the **supremacy** of **white people** over **African Americans** with the use of **terror** and **intimidation**. The Klan **attacked black schools, churches** and **politicians**. Its **membership grew rapidly** to approximately **500 000** by **1871**.

4) **Officials** in the **South** also introduced a range of measures to **stop African Americans** from **voting**, such as the **poll tax** (which required people to **pay** a **tax** before voting) and **literacy tests**. They also brought in a range of **laws** (known as **'Jim Crow' laws**) to **keep** the **races separate**. For example, white and black people had to use **separate schools**, **restaurants**, **parks** and even **drinking fountains**.

Things improved for African Americans after the Civil War — it didn't last...

When people refer to 'the South', they're not only referring to the geographical south of the US, but also to an area that is culturally different from the rest of the US. In this period, the South is associated with segregation and social conservatism.

Background Information on Civil Rights

Now you've got a bit of background on America's history, it'd be useful to get to know America's political system. It's a bit tricky to understand, so you could either watch seven series of 'The West Wing', or just read this page...

The **US Political System** is split into **Three Branches**

In **1787** the **US Constitution** was **created**. It **defined** the **rights**, **duties** and **structure** of the **American government**. The Constitution **split** the government into **three branches** — the **executive**, the **legislature** and the **judiciary**.

1) The **president** (executive) — **runs** the **country**, **recommends legislation** to **Congress**, can issue **Executive Orders** which **don't** require Congress's approval, is the **head** of **state** and the **commander** of the **armed forces**.
2) **Congress** (legislature) — the **US's parliament**, which is split into **two bodies**, the **House of Representatives** and the **Senate**. **Bills** are discussed in Congress. If Congress votes **in favour** of a **bill**, it becomes an **act** — which is a **law**.
3) The **Supreme Court** (judiciary) — the Supreme Court is the **highest court** in the US, which means that in some cases people can **appeal rulings** in **local courts** and have the **Supreme Court** rule upon them — the Supreme Court's rulings are **final**. The Supreme Court can **declare** whether a law is **unconstitutional** (breaks the Constitution) and can **overturn** it. **Supreme Court judges** are **appointed** by the president.

Constitutional Amendments gave **African Americans** some **Legal Rights**

After the **Civil War** (see p.2) **amendments** were **added** to the **Constitution** to give **African Americans legal rights**.

Thirteenth Amendment (1865)
Formally **abolished slavery throughout** the US.

Fourteenth Amendment (1868)
Extended **citizenship** to everyone **born** in the **US** — including **ex-slaves**.

Fifteenth Amendment (1870)
Gave **all male citizens** the **right** to **vote regardless** of their **race**.

The **US** is a **Federation** of **States**

1) Each **state** in the US has its **own government**, **laws** and **legal system**. The head of a state is the **governor**, who is in charge of things such as the **state's budget** and the **state's National Guard** (reserve army).
2) Different states have different laws — for example, **Southern states** had **Jim Crow** (segregation) **laws**.
3) The **federal government** has powers **above** that of **states**. It's responsible for **national defence** and the **prosecution** of some **serious crimes**. The **president** can also **take command** of a **state's National Guard** from the **state governor**.
4) The **Supreme Court** can force states to **scrap laws** it considers **unconstitutional**. **Civil rights activists** tried to get **Supreme Court rulings** to **rid** the **South** of **Jim Crow laws**. If states try to **keep unconstitutional** laws then the **president** can **intervene** to make them **comply** with the **Supreme Court's ruling**.

There are **Two Main Parties** in the US — **Republicans** and **Democrats**

1) The **Republican Party** was **traditionally** based in the **North**. Republicans favour **less federal government intervention** in **people's lives**.
2) The **Democratic Party** had historically been the party of the **South** and the **large industrial cities** of the **North**. Democrat voters were usually **working class**, and in the South the Democrats were supported by **pro-segregationists**. The Democrats believe that the **federal government** should play a **bigger role** in helping **less well-off citizens**.

Ugh — all this learning is affecting my constitution...

The stuff on this page might not seem relevant to the civil rights movement, but it's all really important. The powers of federal government and states, the constitution and the political system in America had a major effect on the campaign for civil rights.

Background Information on Civil Rights

Plessy v Ferguson was a blow to civil rights in America as it denied African Americans the basic rights that they had in the Constitution. African Americans didn't take it lying down, though — they began to organise themselves to fight back.

Plessy v Ferguson Ruled that Segregation was Legal

Southern states had a number of Jim Crow laws which **segregated** the **South** and **prevented** African Americans from **voting**. In **1896**, **African Americans** were dealt a **huge blow** by the **Supreme Court** in the case **Plessy v Ferguson**.

1) **Homer Plessy** deliberately sat in a **whites-only train carriage** and was **arrested**. Plessy **appealed** against his **conviction**, claiming that **segregated transport violated** the **Fourteenth Amendment**.
2) The **Supreme Court** ruled that '**racial segregation** was in the **nature of things**', and that segregation was **legal** as long as the **state** provided '**separate but equal**' facilities for the two races.

Civil Rights Activists fought for the Rights of African Americans

1) **W.E.B. Dubois** was a leading **civil rights** activist in the **early 20th century**. He thought that black people needed to **unite** into a **single organisation** to campaign **peacefully** for change. He helped to create the **National Association for the Advancement of Colored People** (**NAACP**) in **1909** (see p.10).
2) The **NAACP** used **legal tactics** (i.e. using the courts) to challenge aspects of **segregation** in the **South**.
3) **Marcus Garvey** was a **black nationalist** who believed that black people should be **proud** of their **race** and should **live separately** from **other races**. He formed the **Universal Negro Improvement Association** (**UNIA**), which aimed to unite black people, **improve** their **economic conditions** and create an **independent black state**. **Garvey's actions** gained him a **large following** in the **1920s** and led to a growth in **black nationalism** (see p.26).

There was a Great Migration to the North

1) During the **First World War** and the **1920s**, **hundreds** of **thousands** of **African Americans** left the **South** and **settled** in **Northern cities** looking for **work** and **better way** of **life**. This was known as the '**Great Migration**'.
2) In the **North** there was **little legal segregation**, **black workers** received **higher wages** than in the **South**, and it was much **easier** for **African Americans** to **vote**.
3) However, there was still **discrimination** in the **North** — **African Americans** often **lived** in **ghettos** (see glossary p.29), **separate** from other races, where the **housing** and **facilities** were **poor**. **African Americans** were often given **poorly paid jobs** and were **overlooked** in **favour** of **white workers**.

The Second World War Motivated African Americans to Fight Racism at Home

1) In the Second World War **black soldiers** fought in **segregated units** — they **resented** the fact that they had to **fight** for **freedom** in other countries when they **weren't free** in their **own country**.
2) During the war, civil rights activist **A. Philip Randolph** threatened to organise a **march on Washington** to **protest against segregation** in the **army** and **racial discrimination** in **federal employment**. **President Franklin D. Roosevelt** reluctantly issued an **Executive Order** that **banned discrimination** in **federal employment**. He set up a **Commission** to ensure that his orders were carried out.
3) In **1942** the ***Pittsburgh Courier***, a black newspaper, came up with the **slogan 'Double V'**. The paper called for **African Americans** to **fight** for **victory** against **racism abroad** and at **home** in the **US**.

Practice Questions

Q1 What rights did the Fourteenth and Fifteenth Amendments guarantee?

Q2 Why was the outcome of Plessy v Ferguson a set-back for African American civil rights?

The campaign for Civil Rights didn't start in 1945...

Well, all that should give you some decent background information to the module. The US Constitution, the Jim Crow laws and Plessy v Ferguson each have a major part to play, so keep an eye out for them...

Introduction to Section 1

Ahh... my favourite — intro pages. These pages are here to provide you with the key dates, key people and historical vocab that you'll need to ace the exam. In my day we had to make do with revising from long, boring books...

*Here's a **Quick Summary** of **Section One***

This section deals with the **civil rights movement** between **1945** and **1955**. Here's what you need to know:

- The **Second World War** led to some **major changes** for **African Americans**, but they were still **treated badly**. **President Truman** decided to **secure civil rights** for **African Americans.**
- The **President's Committee on Civil Rights** published a **report** in **1947** called **'To Secure These Rights'**. The report stated that **racism** in America was **harmful**, and **suggested** ways in which it could be **tackled**.
- The **National Association for the Advancement of Colored People** (**NAACP**) **challenged segregation** in the **Supreme Court** and won some **important victories.** The most important victory was in the case **Brown v Board of Education of Topeka**. The Supreme Court ruled that **segregation** in **schools** and the **principle** of **'separate but equal'** were **unconstitutional.**
- Members of the **Congress of Racial Equality** (**CORE**) went on the **Journey of Reconciliation** to show that the **Supreme Court's ruling** on **Morgan v Virginia** (which stated that **segregation** on **interstate bus travel contradicted** the **Fourteenth Amendment**) wasn't being **enforced**. They were met with **violence**.

*Learn the **Key Dates** of the **Civil Rights Movement, 1945-1955***

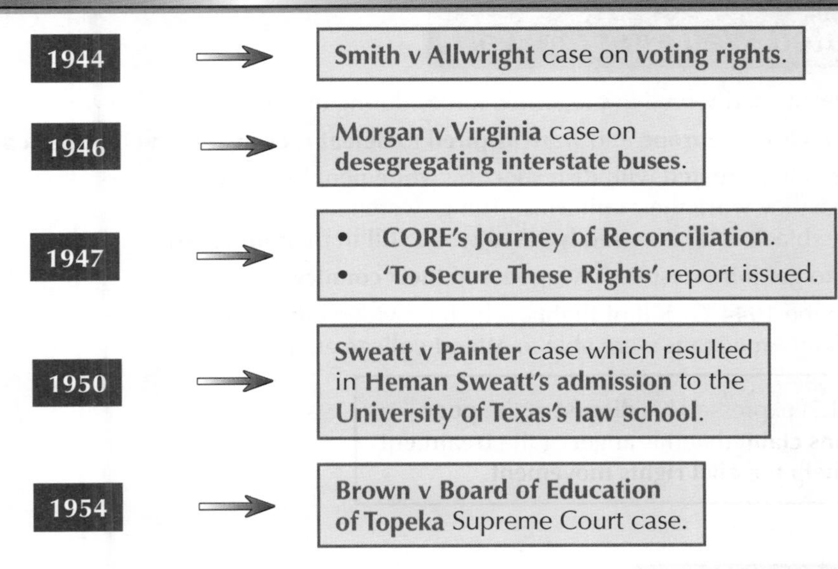

1944 → **Smith v Allwright** case on **voting rights.**

1946 → **Morgan v Virginia** case on **desegregating interstate buses.**

1947 →
- **CORE's Journey of Reconciliation.**
- **'To Secure These Rights'** report issued.

1950 → **Sweatt v Painter** case which resulted in **Heman Sweatt's admission** to the **University of Texas's law school.**

1954 → **Brown v Board of Education of Topeka** Supreme Court case.

Important People in this Period:

- **President Franklin D. Roosevelt** — US President, 1933-1945.
- **President Harry S. Truman** — US President, 1945-1953.
- **President Dwight D. Eisenhower** — US President, 1953-1961.
- **Thurgood Marshall** — Chief Counsel of the NAACP.
- **Earl Warren** — Chief Justice of the Supreme Court, 1953-1969.
- **Emmett Till** — 14-year-old African American boy murdered in 1955.

*Make sure you know what these **Historical Terms** mean*

- **NAACP** — The National Association for the Advancement of Colored People. A civil rights organisation which used legal tactics and the Supreme Court to achieve equality for African Americans.
- **'Separate but equal'** — A principle set down in the Supreme Court ruling on Plessy v Ferguson. It permitted segregation, provided that facilities for white and non-white people were equal.
- **'To Secure These Rights'** — A report published by the President's Committee on Civil Rights (set up by Truman). It condemned racism and recommended ways in which it could be tackled.
- **Direct action** — Where activists tried to directly confront segregation in society with tactics such as sit-ins.
- **CORE** — The Congress of Racial Equality was an African American organisation which used direct action to oppose segregation.
- **Journey of Reconciliation** — Black and white CORE members travelled together to show that the Supreme Court's ruling outlawing segregation on interstate buses was being ignored.
- **Brown v Board of Education of Topeka** — Supreme Court case which ruled that segregation in education was unconstitutional.

Change for African Americans, 1945-1955

The Second World War was the cause of some major changes in America. The fight against the Nazis helped to demonstrate that the problem of racism and white supremacy needed to be addressed in the US.

In the years **1945-55** there were big **Economic** and **Social Changes** in America

1) During the war many African Americans had **left** the **Southern countryside** to work in **towns** and **cities** in the **South**. On top of this, **more than** a **million** African Americans **migrated north** to work in the **new factories**. The **migration** was so great that by **1945** nearly **50%** of African Americans lived in **towns** and **cities**.
2) **Millions** of **African Americans** found **jobs** in the **new factories** built during the war. The factories produced things like **tanks** and **trucks**, which were needed to **win** the **war**.
3) This push towards industrial employment was increased by the use of more **machinery** in **farming**, which resulted in **less demand** for **labourers** to work on the fields. Agricultural work, **especially** picking **cotton**, was the **main** source of jobs for **African Americans**.
4) African Americans who worked in **factories** in the **North** received **higher pay** than they'd done as **farm labourers** in the **South**, but they had **little prospect** of working in more **highly skilled jobs**.
5) The **African Americans** who **migrated** to the cities began to develop their own **communities** and **cultural life**, which centred on their **churches** and other institutions such as **trade unions** and the **National Association for the Advancement of Colored People** (**NAACP**) (see p.4).
6) The **urbanisation** of African Americans helped them to **work together** to **campaign** for their **rights**, as they were gathered **closer together** into **larger communities**.

Black servicemen **Weren't Treated Well** after the war

1) Approximately **one million African Americans** had served in the armed forces during the **Second World War**.
2) Black servicemen saw the effects of **Nazi racism** in **Europe** and were **inspired** to **defeat racism** at **home** in **America**.
3) Black soldiers returning from the war were often **treated** with **disrespect** by **white people** — there were instances where they were **beaten** because they **wore** their **uniforms**. Things weren't so bad as they were after the **First World War** when some black veterans were **lynched** while **still** in their **uniforms**.
4) **Many black ex-servicemen** found it **hard** to **get jobs**, despite having **served their country**.
5) However, **black veterans** did **benefit** from the **1944 GI Bill of Rights**, which provided **education grants** for **ex-servicemen**. As a result, many African Americans were able to **attend college** after the war.

In **1946 President Truman** (see pages 8 and 9) expressed his **disgust** at the **poor treatment** of **black veterans**. **Some historians claim** that this **anger** at the **treatment** of **black ex-servicemen** made him want to **help** the **civil rights movement**.

Segregation was **Enforced** in the **South**

1) Jim Crow laws in the South (see pages 2 and 4) segregated facilities such as **schools**, **parks** and **transport**. This meant that **African Americans** had to **drink** from **separate water fountains**, eat at **separate restaurants** and use **separate toilets**. On **buses** they were **required** to **sit** at the **back** of the **bus** and **give up** their **seats** to **white passengers** if there were no seats free.
2) The **facilities** that were **provided** for **African Americans** were often **under-funded** and of **poor quality**.
3) Many African Americans **accepted** this **inequality** because they felt **powerless** to challenge it. African Americans who **challenged discrimination** in the South faced **arrest**, the **loss** of their **jobs** with white employers, and **violence** from groups such as the **Ku Klux Klan** (see p.2).
4) In the **North**, **segregation** laws were **less common** and **African Americans** could **legally live**, **work** and **vote** alongside white Americans. However, in reality, African Americans faced **discrimination** as they were often **concentrated** in **areas** with **poor housing**, were **overlooked** for **jobs** in favour of **white people** and were **prevented** from joining many **trade unions**.

Change for African Americans, 1945-1955

Between 1945 and 1955 there were some improvements for African Americans, but major problems continued to exist. African Americans were prevented from voting, and most black children continued to receive a lower quality education.

African Americans were often **Denied** their **Right** to **Vote**

1) In the **South** most **African Americans** were **prevented** from **voting** by a **range** of **methods** including **expensive poll taxes**, **intimidation** and the requirement to pass **unfair literacy tests**.
2) Only people who were **registered** to **vote** could be **selected** for **jury service**. This meant **African Americans** who ended up **in court** often faced **injustice**, as they were presented with **all-white juries**.
3) During the war, many African Americans had **challenged Southern officials** by **registering** to **vote**, and by **1952 over one million** African Americans were **registered** in the South. However, in many areas of the **South** the **vast majority** of African Americans were still **prevented** from **voting** in **1955**.
4) In the **North**, **black voters** comprised a **significant percentage** of the **electorate** in **some states**.
5) There were **so many** new **black voters** in the North that **shrewd politicians** tried to **appeal** to them. If **African Americans voted** in a **bloc** (voted **together**) for the **same candidate** then their votes could **determine** the **result** of an **election**.
6) The **impact** of **black voters** can be seen in the **election** of **black Congressman Adam Clayton Powell**, **Jr**., in **1944**. **Black voters** were also **crucial** to **President Truman's re-election** in **1948**.

Education Improved for African Americans, but **Inequalities Continued**

1) Education followed the principle of '**separate but equal**' (see p.5), which meant that **African-American children** were **educated** in **separate schools** to **white children**.
2) On average **Southern states** spent **less than half** as much on **educating black children** as on **white children**.
3) **Spending** on **black schools** in the South **rose rapidly** after the war and many of the **old**, **wooden** and **insanitary schools** were **replaced** with **modern brick buildings**. This **increase** in **spending** was partly done to **encourage African Americans** to **stay** and **work** in the **South** — there was a **shortage** of **labour** due to **migration** to the North.
4) There were some **excellent black schools** and **universities**. For example, **Howard University**, where **Thurgood Marshall** (see p.10) studied law, was open to all **races** and provided a **high standard** of **education**.
5) The **Supreme Court ruled against segregation** in **schools** in the 1954 **Brown v Board of Education case** (see p.12).

Civil Rights was still a **Long Way Off**

1) In many ways, the **situation** of **African Americans** had **improved** in the decade after the **Second World War**. For example, the African Americans who **moved North** in general received **better treatment** and had **better paid jobs**, while in the **South** more **African Americans** were **registered** to **vote** and **black schools** received **more funding**.
2) However, with **legal segregation** still **enforced** in the **South**, and with **social** and **economic segregation** in the **North**, the situation for **African Americans** was still a **long way off** of **full equality** and **full civil rights**.
3) The **period 1945-55** was marked by the **struggle** to **end legal segregation** and to get those in power to admit that **racism** was both **wrong** and **harmful** to **American society**.

Practice Questions

Q1 To what extent did the Second World War improve the status of African Americans?

Q2 What is segregation?

Glossary

lynching — an unlawful execution.

America — everyone's equal, but some are more equal than others...

The 1940s were a period of change for African Americans and there were some improvements in race relations. Unfortunately though, racial discrimination was commonplace and it would take a major change in people's attitudes to achieve civil rights.

'To Secure These Rights'

Truman was a Democrat and he supported civil rights, but the majority of the Southern politicians in his party were segregationists. This made it very difficult for Truman to pass any laws to improve the life of African Americans.

Truman was an **Unlikely Hero** for **Civil Rights**

1) President Harry S. Truman came from the **mid-western** state of **Missouri**, which **enforced segregation**. In **private** Truman was known to use **racist** and **offensive language** about **black people**, **Jews**, **Hispanics** and **Italians**, but as president he tried to **improve** the **status** of **African Americans**.
2) Truman became president in **April 1945** and he made **civil rights** an **important issue**. This may have been because he realised the **importance** of **black voters** (see p.7), but Truman also seems to have genuinely **believed** that the **poor treatment** of African Americans was **unacceptable**.
3) After 1945 the **Cold War** developed, as the **US** and the **Soviet Union** competed **economically** and **politically** to **increase** their **influence** and **support** across the world. **Soviet propaganda** criticised the **poor treatment** of **African Americans** in the US.
4) **Truman** wanted the **Soviet Union** to allow **free** and **fair elections** in the countries of **Eastern Europe occupied** by the **Soviet Union's army**. However, he found it hard to **demand free elections** when this **freedom** was **denied** to **millions** of **African Americans**. Many Americans felt that **civil rights** had to be addressed in the US before they could **criticise** other countries' **lack** of **respect** for **human rights**.

Many members of **Congress** were **Opposed** to civil rights legislation

1) Truman knew that it would be **very difficult** to **pass civil rights measures** into **law**.
2) **Congress** included a large number of **Southern Representatives** and **Senators**, mainly from the **Democratic Party**, who were **hostile** to **civil rights**, and they were **supported** by some **Northern Republicans**. In **1948** some **Southern Democrats** formed the **'Dixiecrats'** — a **pro-segregationist** party. They ran in the **1948 presidential election** and won **2.4%** of the **national vote**.
3) **Opponents** to **civil rights** in **Congress** used **tactics** like **filibustering** to **block civil rights legislation**. **Filibustering** is where **congressmen work together** to **use up** all the **time available** to **debate** a **bill** by giving long speeches. This can **prevent** a bill from becoming a **law**.
4) Congress even **blocked** attempts to introduce a **federal anti-lynching law** because they claimed it would **interfere** with the **rights** of **individual states**.
5) Truman **bypassed Congress** with **Executive Orders** to **improve rights** for **African Americans** (see p.9).

Truman set up the **President's Committee on Civil Rights**

1) In **December 1946** Truman signed an **Executive Order** announcing the creation of a **presidential commission** which would **investigate** the ways in which the **rights** of **African Americans** were being **violated**.
2) The Committee was to **report back** to the President **within** a **year**. In **December 1947** the Committee issued their **report** entitled **'To Secure these Rights'**.
3) **'To Secure These Rights'** clearly stated that **racism** was **harmful** to the **country** and **not** in keeping with what **America** should **stand for** — **freedom** and **equality**.
4) **Over** a **million copies** of the **report** were **printed** by the **US government** and **private publishers**, and it was widely discussed in **newspapers** and on the **radio**.

© Everett Collection/Rex Features

African American man drinking from a 'colored' water cooler in 1939.

5) In **January 1948** Truman gave his **State of the Union address** to **Congress**. In it he stated that he was going to secure the **"essential human rights** of our **citizens"**. Truman also argued that **racial discrimination**, especially in **education**, in the **workplace** and at the **voting booths** was **"contrary** to **American ideals** of **democracy"**.

'To Secure These Rights'

Truman's decision to speak out on civil rights was a brave one, especially in a presidential election year. A poll taken in March 1948 showed that 82% of Americans opposed Truman's civil rights policies. Truman wasn't deterred. No siree...

'To Secure These Rights' attacked **Racism** in **Several Ways**

1) '**To Secure These Rights**' detailed the **extent** of **racial discrimination** in **American society**. African Americans were **subjected** to **injustices** like **police brutality** and **lynching**. Lynching was **illegal**, but many of those who were **tried** for **lynching** were **acquitted** by **all-white juries**, and it was often **condoned** by **state law enforcement officials**.
2) The **report attacked** the **many problems** that **racism** caused:

- **Denying citizens** the **right** to **vote undermined US democracy** and the **principles** of **freedom** and **equality**.
- Discrimination against **African Americans** had a **negative effect** on the country's **economy**. **Segregation** led to **money** being **wasted** on **two sets** of **facilities**, and because African Americans were **poorly paid** they **couldn't** buy **consumer goods**, which **hurt** US **industry**.
- **Racism** in the **US** was **criticised** by the US's **opponents** abroad and **damaged relations** with **America's allies**.
- The US was seen as hypocritical in its support for **decolonisation** in countries like **India** and **Pakistan** (which became **independent** in **1947**) as it continued **denying rights** to **black people** in the US.

3) The **report called for**:

- **Federal anti-lynching laws** to be passed, which meant **federal authorities** could **prosecute** those involved, including **officers of the law** who had **failed** to **protect** African Americans.
- **Fair employment laws** to be **tightened** to **prevent racial discrimination**.
- The **federal government** to take action to **ensure** black people could **vote** in all **state** and **national elections**.
- Action to be taken to **prevent police brutality** against African Americans.

Congress Blocked any **Progress** on **Civil Rights**

1) Truman **welcomed** the **report**, but was **unable** to **take action** on most of its recommendations because **Congress** was **opposed** to many of the **reforms**.
2) Truman remained in office until **1953**, but in the **later years** of his **presidency** his **attention** was **diverted** to **foreign affairs** — **notably** the **Korean War** (**1950-53**). This meant that progress on **civil rights stalled**.
3) However, **Truman** used **Executive Orders** (which **didn't** need **Congress's approval**) to **force change** in some areas:

- **Executive Order 9980** set up the **Fair Employment Board**. It enforced **equal opportunities** in **government organisations**, but it didn't have enough **funding** to **operate properly**.
- **Executive Order 10308** withheld **defence contracts** from firms which practised **discrimination**. It set up the **Committee on Government Contract Compliance** (**CGCC**) to **monitor** the awarding of **government contracts**.
- **Executive Order 9981** called for **racial equality** in the **armed forces**. Some officers were **reluctant** to carry out this order, but a **shortage** of **troops** during the **Korean War** meant that units **couldn't** be **segregated**.

Practice Question

Q1 Give two examples of reforms suggested by the President's Committee report 'To Secure These Rights'.

Glossary

State of the Union address — a speech given by the president to Congress, which sets out his policies. It happens once a year, usually in January.

Cold War — a period of hostility and rivalry between the US and the Soviet Union which lasted from the end of the Second World War until 1991.

Executive Order 1138 — have a biscuit after revising...

Truman's decision to support the civil rights movement put civil rights at the forefront of American politics and meant that it could no longer be ignored. Truman's support gave him the black vote, which helped him win the very close 1948 presidential election.

The Work of the NAACP

The National Association for the Advancement of Colored People (NAACP) was created to fight for the civil rights of black people, and in the decade after the war it achieved some important successes. So you gotta revise them. Hooray!

The **NAACP** was founded to **Fight Discrimination**

1) The **NAACP** was **founded** in **1909** by **W.E.B. Dubois** and other civil rights activists. They wanted to **unite African Americans** into a **single organisation** to **peacefully campaign** for **change** in the **US**.
2) The NAACP aimed to **challenge segregation** in the **courts**. They hoped to secure **legal equality** for **African Americans** so that they **couldn't** be **treated differently** from **white US citizens**.
3) In **some cases** the NAACP used **other tactics**, such as **protests** and **boycotts**, to **highlight** certain **inequalities**.
4) NAACP membership **wasn't** restricted to African Americans — many of its members were **white** — but its campaigns focused on **African Americans**.
5) **Membership** of the **NAACP** grew **significantly** during the **Second World War**, and the organisation had about **450 000** members by **1945**. This allowed the **NAACP** to become **more active** in campaigning for civil rights.

The **NAACP** used the **US Constitution** to advance **Civil Rights**

1) The **NAACP** tried to get the US government to **honour** the **Fourteenth** and **Fifteenth Amendments** (see p.3) of the **US Constitution**. The Supreme Court had declared segregation legal in the **judgement** on **Plessy v Ferguson** (see p.4), so the **NAACP** aimed to **persuade** the **Supreme Court** to **reverse** its earlier decision and **force** Southern states to **repeal** their **Jim Crow** laws.
2) The **NAACP provided funding** and **lawyers** for **individuals** to bring cases **against** the **authorities**.
3) The **NAACP** also tried to **raise awareness** of their **cause** — they **appealed** to **politicians** in **Washington** for backing, **encouraged African Americans** to **register** to **vote**, and **organised** and **supported protests**.
4) Some African Americans felt that the NAACP's **methods** were **too slow** and that they **didn't** change people's **attitudes**. The **NAACP wasn't** completely **opposed** to taking **direct action** to challenge racism, but felt that **widespread** and **lasting change** could **only happen** through the **Supreme Court**.

Thurgood Marshall was a leading **Civil Rights Lawyer**

1) **Thurgood Marshall**, an African American, was one of the **NAACP's** most **successful lawyers**.
2) In **1938** Marshall became **chief counsel** for the **NAACP**. He **won** several **important cases** on **racial discrimination**, including **Smith v Allwright**, **Morgan v Virginia** and **Sweatt v Painter** (see p.11). Marshall **won 29** of the **32 cases** he brought before the **Supreme Court**.
3) In **1967 Marshall** was **nominated** to the **Supreme Court** by **President Lyndon B. Johnson**. Marshall **served** on the **Supreme Court** between **1967** and **1991**.

- In the early **1950s Marshall** and **other NAACP leaders** started to plan a **major attack** on **segregation** in **schools**.
- **Throughout** the **1940s** the **Supreme Court** had issued a number of decisions **against segregation**. However, **Marshall wouldn't act** until he could be fairly **sure** of success — **failure** might **set back** the **civil rights movement** by **many years**.
- The opportunity to act arose when, in **1953**, **President Dwight D. Eisenhower** appointed **Earl Warren** (see p.12) as **Chief Justice of the Supreme Court**.

Thurgood Marshall

The Work of the NAACP

The NAACP won some important victories in the Supreme Court, but it wasn't the only civil rights organisation to come to prominence after the war. The Congress of Racial Equality (CORE) also aimed to challenge segregation peacefully.

There were several **Legal Challenges** to **Segregation** between **1944** and **1950**

Smith v Allwright — 1944

1) **Lonnie Smith** wanted to **vote** in the **Democrats' primary election** in **Texas**, but was **denied** the chance to vote because he was black.
2) A **primary election** is where a **political party's members choose** their **candidate** for an **election**. **Primary elections** were **important** in **Texas** because the **Democratic Party** was often the **only party** with a **chance** of winning, so the primary was the **only meaningful election** in the state.
3) **Thurgood Marshall** argued Smith's case and the **Supreme Court** ruled that white-only **primary elections violated** the **Fifteenth Amendment**.

Morgan v Virginia — 1946

1) **Irene Morgan refused** to **give up her seat** to a **white passenger** while **travelling** on an **interstate bus** in **Virginia**. She was **fined**.
2) Marshall argued her case and the **Supreme Court** declared that **segregation** on **interstate buses** broke the **Fourteenth Amendment**.

Sweatt v Painter — 1950

1) **Heman Sweatt**, a black student, was **refused admission** to the **law school** at the **University of Texas**. The **NAACP** and Marshall took his case to the **Supreme Court**.
2) **Before** the case was heard a **separate law school** for African Americans was **hurriedly** built. However, the **Supreme Court** ruled that the new law school provided an **inferior education** and **poor facilities**, and that **Sweatt** should be **admitted** to the **University of Texas law school**.

These Supreme Court judgements **provided legal** (**de jure**) **support** for **desegregation**, but it was **very difficult** to ensure that these decisions were **put into practice** to secure **real** (**de facto**) **change**.

CORE took a more **Direct Approach** than the **NAACP**

1) The Congress of Racial Equality (**CORE**) was created in **1942**. It was a civil rights organisation set up to **oppose segregation** — especially in **restaurants** and **interstate transport**.
2) **Unlike** the **NAACP**, **CORE** strongly advocated **direct action**. In **1947**, **CORE** members undertook the **Journey of Reconciliation**. **Black** and **white** members **travelled together** on **interstate buses** in the **South** to show that the **Supreme Court's** ruling on **Morgan v Virginia wasn't** being **enforced**.
3) The **NAACP denounced** the **Journey of Reconciliation**, because it **feared** that **CORE's actions** would lead to **violence**, but it promised **legal assistance** to CORE members.
4) The **Journey of Reconciliation revealed** that Southern states were **ignoring** the **Supreme Court's ruling** against segregation on interstate buses. **Two black members** of **CORE** were sentenced to **thirty days** in **jail** and two of the **white members** were sentenced to **three months** in **jail** for refusing to sit in separate sections of the bus.
5) The **Journey of Reconciliation failed** to make any changes in the South, but it provided a lot of **publicity** for **CORE**, which **continued** its policies of **peaceful direct action** throughout the **1950s**.

Practice Question

Q1 How did the NAACP try to get the US government to honour the Fourteenth and Fifteenth Amendments?

Glossary

de jure — something which is stated in law. This doesn't necessarily mean that the law is obeyed in reality.

de facto — something which happens in practice, regardless of any laws.

So many acronyms to learn — it makes me sick to my CORE...

The Supreme Court made some important rulings in this period thanks to the NAACP's work in highlighting the contradictions between segregation and the Constitution. CORE's peaceful protests also had a huge influence on the civil rights movement.

Brown v Board of Education

Brown v Board of Education of Topeka (to give its full title) is probably the most famous Supreme Court case in this period. The case was a challenge to the whole system of segregation and it was a crucial victory for the NAACP.

Brown v Board of Education was Very Important

1) **Oliver Brown** lived in **Topeka**, **Kansas**, a town where **most facilities**, including **schools**, were **segregated**. He lived just **a few blocks** from an **all-white school** which had **refused** to **admit** his 7-year-old **daughter Linda**.
2) As a result, **Linda** had to **travel** across town **on her own** — **crossing** a **railway line** and **several busy streets** to go to a school for African Americans.
3) **Marshall** and the **NAACP** decided to take Brown's case to the **Supreme Court** in the hope of **overturning** the practice of **segregation** in **education**.

The Supreme Court ruling

- In May 1954 the **Supreme Court** made a **unanimous** judgement — **segregated schools violated** the **Fourteenth Amendment**. The Court ruled that **all** children should have access to their **local school**, **regardless** of their **colour**. The Court **completely rejected** the **principle** of **'separate but equal'** set down by **Plessy v Ferguson**.
- **Earl Warren**, Chief Justice of the Supreme Court, played a **key role** in **convincing** the other **Supreme Court judges** to **end segregation** in **education** and in securing a **unanimous verdict** from the judges.
- The **Court** ruled that **black schools** were **not equal** to **white schools** — they offered a **lower quality** of **education**, which ensured that most of their pupils would go on to get **low-skilled, poorly paid** jobs.
- The Court also argued that segregation was **"inherently unequal"** as even if black schools were of equal quality, the fact of being segregated had **harmful psychological effects** on **young African Americans**, making them feel **inferior**.

Chief Justice Earl Warren in 1956.

4) The **Warren Court** (the Supreme Court named after its Chief Justice) was a **strong supporter** of civil rights. **Earl Warren's liberal influence** was a key factor in **securing legal rights** for African Americans.

The NAACP was Victorious... but the Battle Wasn't Over

1) The **decision** in the **Brown case** was hailed as being a **more important step** towards **equal rights** for African Americans than **'To Secure These Rights'**. It was also the **greatest triumph** of **Thurgood Marshall's career**.
2) **Marshall's victory** led many **African Americans** to try to **challenge** other aspects of **segregation**, believing that the **Supreme Court** would **rule** in their **favour**. The **NAACP** and **CORE increased** their **voter registration campaigns** and **protests against segregation**.
3) However, although there was now a **legal** (de jure) **ruling demanding** the **integration** of **schools**, this **didn't automatically** lead to the de facto **desegregation** of **schools** in the **South**.

The Progress of Desegregation was Slow

1) After the **Supreme Court issued** its **decision**, **some** school districts **immediately obeyed** the **ruling**. However, **many states** simply **refused** to **accept** the **ruling**, and **progress** was **slow**.
2) **One reason** for the **slow progress** towards integrated schools was that the **Court** hadn't **set** any **timescale** for **obeying** its **ruling**, so **states** and **schools took their time**.
3) Many **white parents** wanted to **keep segregated schools** — they decided to **resist** the **Court's decision**.

Brown v Board of Education

Unsurprisingly, opponents of civil rights didn't take the Supreme Court's decision lying down and there was a backlash against desegregation. In many cases, the Supreme Court's ruling was simply ignored. Eisenhower didn't help either.

The White Citizens' Council led the Opposition to Desegregation

1) The **White Citizens' Council** (later known as the **Citizens' Councils of America**) was a **white supremacist organisation** that attracted membership among the **leading members** of **white communities**. The council organised a **propaganda campaign** in the South **against** integrated education and pressured employers to **sack** civil rights activists. **Formed** in **1954**, they had over **250 000 members** within **two years**.
2) The **Southern Manifesto**, written in 1956, rejected the **Supreme Court's ruling** in **Brown v Board of Education** and called for **"lawful" opposition** to **desegregation**. It was **signed** by **101 Southern Congressmen**.
3) By the end of **1956 six Southern states** had **blocked** any attempts to **desegregate schools**. In **Virginia** a campaign called '**massive resistance**' was launched by **Senator Harry F. Byrd**. To **avoid desegregation**, local authorities **shut** their **schools** or **passed laws** which **cut funding** to **desegregated schools**.
4) The **1950s** also saw a **rise** in the membership of the **Ku Klux Klan** (see p.2). The **Klan** used **terrorism** and **violence** to **attack civil rights campaigners** and to **stop desegregation** in the South.
5) Local authorities in the South **threatened** that **NAACP members** would be **sacked**. Many **black teachers resigned** from the **NAACP** to **keep** their **jobs**. **NAACP membership** in the South **fell significantly** in the 1950s.

- This period was marked by the **violent murder** of **Emmett Till**, a 14-year-old African-American boy, in **1955**.
- Till, who was visiting relatives in **Mississippi**, was **abducted**, **beaten** and **shot** for **allegedly flirting** with a **married white woman**. The woman's husband and his half-brother were put on trial for murder — they were **acquitted** by an **all-white jury**. Later, in an **interview**, the **defendants admitted** to **killing Till**.
- Till's murder was **reported** in the **national media** and **sparked outrage** amongst **African Americans** and **white people**. The incident made many people **realise** that **civil rights** was a cause **worth fighting for**.

Eisenhower showed Little Leadership on Civil Rights

1) **Eisenhower** was **president** from **1953** to **1961**. He'd appointed **Earl Warren** as **Chief Justice**, but it was a decision he **regretted**, calling it the **"biggest damned-fool mistake I ever made"**.
2) Eisenhower **didn't** want to use federal power to **force desegregation** as he felt it would **stir up trouble**. He believed that **de facto change** would **take time** — **"I don't believe you can change the hearts of men with law or decisions"**.
3) Eisenhower was a **very popular president** — if he'd given **more support** to the **Supreme Court**, the **integration** of **schools** might have been achieved **far sooner**.

The NAACP tried to get a Timetable for Desegregation

1) In **1955** the **NAACP** tried to get the **Supreme Court** to give a **clear timetable** for the **desegregation** of all schools.
2) The **Court** responded with what is known as the **Brown II ruling**. The Court was **unwilling** to **provide** a **timetable** — it was only prepared to declare that **desegregation** should be carried out **"with all deliberate speed"**.
3) **Brown II** was a **disastrous decision** for the **NAACP**. By failing to set a **clear timetable** for the **integration** of **schools**, the **Court encouraged resistance** to its **verdict** in **Brown v Board of Education** across the **South**.

Practice Questions

Q1 Why was Brown v Board of Education such an important victory for the civil rights movement?

Exam Question

Q1 To what extent did the NAACP achieve its aims in the years 1945 to 1955? [30 Marks]

You v Exams — luckily you've got the Supreme CGP on your side...

Brown v Board of Education may have been a momentous occasion in the struggle for civil rights, but very little changed at first. Little Rock, Arkansas, would be where the struggle for school desegregation broke out and attracted national attention (see p.16).

Introduction to Section 2

Dates, important people and historical terms. Make sure you know them. Simple as that.

Here's a **Quick Summary** of **Section Two**

This section deals with the **civil rights movement** in the years **1955-1968**. Here's what you should know:

- During this period, **civil rights activists** took **direct action** to **oppose segregation**. In **1955** in **Montgomery, Alabama**, African Americans organised a **bus boycott** to **protest** against **segregation** on buses. In **1960**, **students** in **Greensboro, North Carolina, campaigned against segregation** in **restaurants**.
- **Martin Luther King** emerged as a **leader** of the **civil rights movement**. In **1963** he led the **successful Birmingham campaign** and gave his famous **'I Have a Dream' speech** in **Washington, D.C.** However, he **wasn't** always successful — e.g. the **Albany movement** in **1961-62** and the **1966 Chicago campaign** both **failed** to **achieve** their **objectives**.
- **President Johnson passed** the **1964 Civil Rights Act** and the **1965 Voting Rights Act**. These laws gave African Americans **full legal rights**.

Learn the **Key Dates** of the **Civil Rights Movement**, 1955-1968

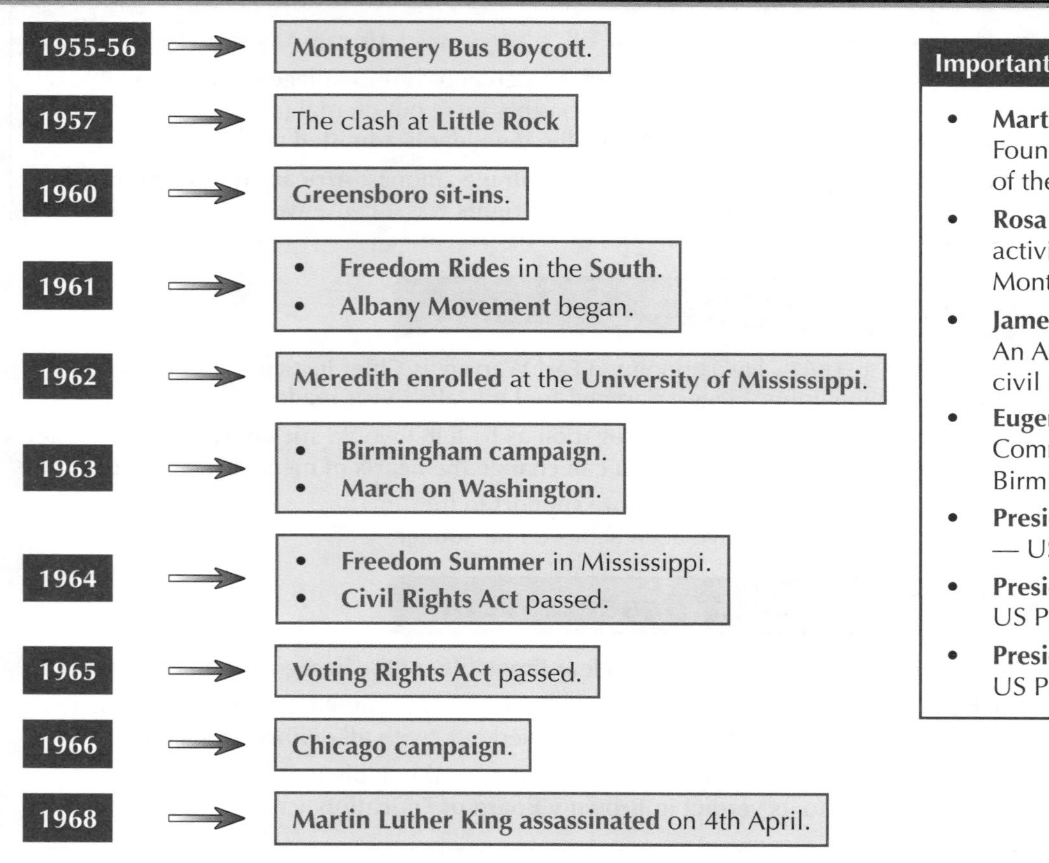

- **1955-56** → **Montgomery Bus Boycott.**
- **1957** → The clash at **Little Rock**
- **1960** → **Greensboro sit-ins.**
- **1961** →
  - **Freedom Rides** in the **South**.
  - **Albany Movement** began.
- **1962** → **Meredith enrolled** at the **University of Mississippi**.
- **1963** →
  - **Birmingham campaign.**
  - **March on Washington.**
- **1964** →
  - **Freedom Summer** in Mississippi.
  - **Civil Rights Act** passed.
- **1965** → **Voting Rights Act** passed.
- **1966** → **Chicago campaign.**
- **1968** → **Martin Luther King assassinated** on 4th April.

Important People in this Period:

- **Martin Luther King, Jr.** — Founder of the SCLC and a leader of the civil rights movement.
- **Rosa Parks** — A civil rights activist who sparked the Montgomery Bus Boycott.
- **James Meredith** — An African-American student and civil rights activist.
- **Eugene 'Bull' Connor** — Commissioner of Public Safety in Birmingham, Alabama.
- **President Dwight D. Eisenhower** — US President, 1953-1961.
- **President John F. Kennedy** — US President, 1961-1963.
- **President Lyndon B. Johnson** — US President, 1963-1969.

Make sure you know what these **Historical Terms** mean

- **SCLC** — The Southern Christian Leadership Conference is a civil rights organisation that was founded by King.
- **SNCC** (pronounced 'snick') — The Student Nonviolent Coordinating Committee was a civil rights organisation created by students.
- **Freedom Rides** — A series of protests where civil rights activists travelled on buses to show that the Supreme Court judgements on segregation weren't being enforced.
- **Sit-ins** — Protests where African Americans occupied whites-only facilities, such as the Greensboro lunch counter.
- **Freedom Summer** — A campaign in the summer of 1964 to help African Americans in Mississippi register to vote.

The Montgomery Bus Boycott

From 1955 the civil rights movement focused on more direct action. The Montgomery Bus Boycott was the first in a number of high-profile campaigns where African Americans directly challenged segregation in the South.

The NAACP wanted to Challenge Segregation on Buses

1) The **NAACP** in **Montgomery**, **Alabama**, wanted to **challenge segregation** on the city's buses. On **buses** in the **South**, **black people** had to sit at the **back** of the bus and **give up their seats** to **white passengers** if there weren't seats available. In Montgomery, **all** bus drivers were **white**, and many **abused** and **insulted** their **black passengers**.
2) On **1st December 1955** Rosa Parks, a local **NAACP member**, **refused** to give up her seat to a **white passenger** and was **arrested**. Black community leaders demanded **direct action** — a **boycott** of the city's buses. To organise this boycott the **Montgomery Improvement Association** (**MIA**) was formed, led by a local **preacher** — **Martin Luther King**, **Jr**. (see pages 20-21).
3) The **MIA** didn't demand the **complete desegregation** of **city buses**, they called for passengers to be seated on a **first-come**, **first-served** basis — **African Americans** would fill seats from the **back** and **white people** from the **front**. They also asked for **black drivers** to be **employed** on bus routes through **black communities**. The city's authorities **refused** to **compromise**, so the **MIA** decided to fight for the **complete desegregation** of city **buses**.

There is **much debate** as to whether **Rosa Parks's refusal** to give up her seat was **preplanned** or a **spontaneous act** of **defiance**. The **NAACP** wanted to **challenge segregation** on **Montgomery's buses** and **Parks**, a **respected member** of the **community**, was an **ideal figurehead** for the campaign. **Claudette Colvin** had **similarly refused** to give up her seat to a **white passenger**, but she was **fifteen**, **pregnant** and **unmarried**, so she wouldn't have been viewed as a such a **safe candidate**.

The Montgomery Bus Boycott was Successful

1) **Most** African Americans in Montgomery **boycotted** (stopped using) the **buses** — many **walked** to and from **work** instead. Some organised a system of **lift sharing**, and **black taxi-drivers** took black passengers at **reduced rates**.
2) The **bus company** was nearly **bankrupted** — it lost **65%** of its **revenue** during the boycott.
3) In their sermons, **King** and other preachers **spoke out** against **segregation** and in **support** of the boycott.
4) The city's authorities **arrested** over **150 protesters** during a march against segregation. **King** was **sentenced** to **one year** in **prison**, but he was **released** after **two weeks** when the **media criticised** his **imprisonment**.
5) The **NAACP's legal challenge** (**Browder v Gayle**) on the **segregation** of **buses** went to a **District Court**, which **ruled against segregation**. This ruling was **appealed** in the **Supreme Court** by the city's lawyers, but the court upheld the ruling in **November 1956**. On **20th December** the **city buses** were **desegregated** and the **boycott ended**.

The Boycott had some Important Consequences

1) The **boycott** showed **African Americans** that if they **worked together** they could achieve **significant results**.
2) It also **highlighted** the **economic power** of **African Americans**. The bus company **nearly collapsed** without the revenue from **black passengers**, and the city's **shops suffered** because African Americans **didn't travel** to them.
3) The **civil rights movement** became **more** than a **series** of **legal challenges** — **activists** were **taking to the streets**.
4) **King** emerged as a **leading figure** in the **civil rights struggle**. He was **determined** to **maintain** the **pressure** for **change**, so he helped to **found** the **Southern Christian Leadership Conference** (**SCLC**). King led the **SCLC** from its founding in **1957** up to his assassination in **1968**.

Practice Question

Q1 In no more than 50 words, explain how African Americans challenged segregation on buses in Montgomery, Alabama.

Racism was Bus-ted in Montgomery...

The Montgomery Bus Boycott was an important learning experience for civil rights activists. It showed that peaceful opposition could get results if African Americans worked together. Martin Luther King used this tactic in his campaigns for civil rights.

Little Rock and Segregation in Education

The clash at Little Rock, Arkansas, was the first major test for the Brown v Board of Education ruling (see p.12). The incident at Little Rock wasn't strictly a protest, but it was part of the campaign to challenge segregation in the South.

There was **Opposition** to **Desegregation** in **Little Rock, Arkansas**

1) Since the **Supreme Court's ruling** on **Brown v Board of Education**, most **Southern authorities** had **refused** to **desegregate** their **schools**. To change this situation the **NAACP** decided to act in **Little Rock**, **Arkansas**.
2) Due to **pressure** from an **NAACP** lawsuit, **ten black students** were allowed to **enrol** at the **prestigious Central High School** in **Little Rock** in **September 1957**. During the **summer** of **1957** the **NAACP** helped to **prepare** the **students** for the **violence** and **intimidation** that they were likely to face at the school.
3) On 2nd September, the day before the school opened, the **governor** of **Arkansas**, **Orval Faubus**, stationed the local **National Guard** (reservist soldiers) **outside** the **school** to **prevent** the **black students** from **entering**. He claimed that he had to **prevent disorder** in the city.
4) Faubus's actions created a **crisis** — **Eisenhower** had to **intervene** to **enforce** the **law**. Eisenhower **ordered** the **National Guard** to **withdraw**, but a **large**, **hostile crowd** of **white people prevented** the **students** from **entering** the **school**. **Eisenhower ordered soldiers** to **return** to the **school** — this time to **protect** the **students** and help them get inside.
5) **One** of the **ten** students **enrolled** at **another school** — the other nine **continued** to **attend** through the **school** year.
6) In the **summer** of **1958 Faubus**, who was running for **re-election** in **1960**, **closed the schools** in **Little Rock** to **avoid integration** — they remained shut for the **entire 1958-59 school year**. A federal court ruled that the closure was **unconstitutional**, and they were **reopened** in September 1959.

Little Rock Proved that **Desegregation** was still a **Long Way Off**

1) **Eisenhower never** spoke **publicly** in **support** of the **Brown v Board of Education judgement**, and he was **unwilling** to **intervene** in **Little Rock**. Eisenhower **didn't** want to **use troops** to **force desegregation**, as it was such an unpopular move in the South, but as president he had to prevent **Faubus** from **breaking federal law**.
2) Eisenhower was **criticised** by **both sides** on the issue of segregation. **Pro-segregationists compared** the **soldiers** used by Eisenhower to **"Hitler's storm troopers"**, while **civil rights activists complained** that his **indecisiveness** showed **extremists** that he **wasn't** committed to civil rights.
3) The events in **Little Rock** showed **African Americans** that **desegregation** would only be achieved **slowly** in the **South**, and that it was **vital** that the **federal government** should **act** to **uphold** the **law**.
4) **Eisenhower** and **Congress** took **no action** to **promote school desegregation** after the Little Rock incident. By **1964** less than **2%** of **black children** in the **South** attended **desegregated schools**.

James Meredith led his own **Campaign Against Segregation** in **Education**

1) In **1961 James Meredith** tried to become the **first** black student to **enrol** at the **University of Mississippi**. He applied to join the **law school**, but was **refused** because of his **race**.
2) The **NAACP** helped Meredith to gain admission to the **University of Mississippi** by securing a **Supreme Court** verdict in his favour.
3) Bowing to pressure from the **Kennedy administration**, **Governor Ross Barnett** allowed **Meredith** to attend the University in **September 1962**, but **refused** to **protect him**.
4) Meredith tried to enter the **university**, but was **prevented** by a **crowd** of **white protestors**. A **riot** broke out in which **two people** were **killed**. **Kennedy** sent **federal troops** to help Meredith enter the **law school**, and he **successfully enrolled** in **October 1962**.
5) **Meredith** was provided with **federal guards** to protect him until he **graduated** the following year. After he graduated he **continued** to **campaign** for **civil rights** and he started his **March Against Fear** in **1966** (see p.30).

James Meredith being escorted by federal marshals as he enrols at the University of Mississippi in October 1962.

The Greensboro Sit-ins

The civil rights movement hadn't been very successful between 1957 and 1960 — but things burst into life with the Greensboro sit-ins. Students and young people became more direct in confronting segregation and had some success.

Students Organised the Greensboro Sit-ins

1) **Four students** from an **agricultural college** in **Greensboro, North Carolina**, decided to **challenge** the policy of **segregated lunch counters** at their local **Woolworth's store**. On **1st February 1960** they sat down in '**whites only**' **seats** and **ordered coffee**. They **weren't served** and were **asked** to **leave**, but they **refused** to **move** and **stayed seated** until the store **closed**. They then **returned** to carry on their **protest** the **next day**.
2) **More students** joined the **four**, and by **6th February over 300 students** jammed the streets around the store.
3) The **Greensboro protest** was **copied throughout** the **South**, with protests made against **segregated public spaces** such as **parks**, **libraries**, **cinemas** and **restaurants**. The **direct action** taken by the students of Greensboro **appealed** to **young people** and roughly **70 000 students participated** in **sit-ins** across the **South**.
4) **Students** in **Nashville, Tennessee**, organised a **campaign** of **sit-ins** and **boycotts** to **desegregate lunch counters**. They **forced local authorities** to **desegregate** not only **lunch counters**, but **other facilities** too.
5) In **July 1960 Woolworth desegregated** its **lunch counters**, and **within** a **year over** a **hundred cities** in the **South** had taken steps to **desegregate** their **facilities**. This seemed to **prove** that **direct action** was **effective**.

The Greensboro Sit-ins Revitalised the Civil Rights Movement

1) **Protests** such as those in **Greensboro** and **Nashville** helped the civil rights movement to gain **momentum**. They showed the power of African Americans **working together** against racism.
2) The sit-ins marked a **new phase** in **peaceful protests** — they were becoming more **organised** and **confrontational**.
3) The **students** acted **independently** of both the **NAACP** and **King's SCLC** — **King** only became **involved** in the **later campaigns**. Some African Americans **criticised King** for his **lack** of **action** and for **not** providing **strong leadership**.
4) With the help of **King** and **financial backing** from the **SCLC**, **some** of the **students involved** in the **protests formed** the **Student Nonviolent Coordinating Committee** (**SNCC**) in **1960**. Its aim was to **organise** and **coordinate** further **peaceful protests**.

Non-violent Direct Action was the Main Tactic of Civil Rights Campaigners

1) The **success** of the **Greensboro sit-ins**, and the **subsequent sit-ins across** the **South**, showed that **non-violent direct action** could **achieve quick** and **widespread change**.
2) Non-violent direct action **appealed** to **young African-American** civil rights campaigners. They felt that the **tactics** of the **NAACP** were **too slow** and only led to **de jure** rather than **de facto change**.
3) King was **inspired** by the **students**' confrontational **non-violent direct action** and applied it to his **own campaigns**.
4) However, **non-violent direct action didn't** always bring success. In many cases its **effectiveness** relied on **provoking violence** from **white people** and using **media publicity** to **pressurise** the **government** to overturn the **Jim Crow laws**. If the **local authorities didn't** respond **violently**, then the campaign **lost publicity** and had limited **ability** to **force improvements** — this happened in **Albany** in **1961-62** (see p.19).

Practice Questions

Q1 Briefly summarise what happened in Little Rock, Arkansas in 1957.

Q2 What were the students in Greensboro, North Carolina, protesting against in 1960?

Q3 Why was non-violent direct action so appealing to African-American civil rights campaigners?

My favourite method of protest — the lie-in...

The defiance shown by the students in Greensboro inspired activists across the country to make a stand against injustice. Their confrontational tactics were more assertive than boycotts and they influenced King to apply their methods to his own campaigns.

The Freedom Rides

Inspired by the success of the sit-ins, CORE decided to try a campaign of their own similar to their 1947 Journey of Reconciliation. The Freedom Rides were met with violence, and splits began to appear in the civil rights movement.

CORE Organised the Freedom Rides

1) **CORE** had **achieved little** since the **Journey of Reconciliation** in **1947** (see p.11), but it was impressed by the **Greensboro sit-ins** and **joined forces** with **SNCC** to **challenge segregation** in **interstate travel**.
2) In **1960** the **Supreme Court ruled** that segregation of **interstate bus terminals** was **unconstitutional** (Boynton v Virginia), so in **1961 CORE** and **SNCC activists** went on **'Freedom Rides'**, to **prove** that this ruling and the **1946 Morgan v Virginia** ruling (see p.11) **weren't** being **enforced** in the **South**. To do this **black activists** sat on **white-only seats** on the **buses** and attempted to use **white-only restaurants** and **facilities** at **bus terminals**.
3) **CORE's leader**, **James Farmer**, hoped that **Southern racists** would **react violently** to the **Freedom Rides** and **create news headlines** which would **damage** the **US's international prestige**. Farmer believed this would **force President Kennedy** to **uphold** the **law** and **desegregate** the **buses**.

- The **Rides began** in **May 1961**. **Much** of the **journey** from **Washington, D.C.**, to the **South** was **peaceful**, but the **Freedom Riders** encountered **fierce resistance** when they **entered Alabama**.
- In **Anniston** their **bus** was **firebombed**, its **tyres** were **slit**, and the **riders** were **savagely beaten**. In **Birmingham** the **Commissioner of Public Safety** (who had authority over the city's police), **Eugene 'Bull' Connor**, **allowed** the **bus** and its **occupants** to be **attacked** by the **Ku Klux Klan**. The **riders** suffered **similar violence** in **Montgomery**.
- **Freedom Rides continued** through the **summer** of **1961**, despite calls by **President Kennedy** to **end** them. **Kennedy** was **worried** about the **effect** the **violence** would have on the **US's standing** in the **world**.
- The **Kennedy Administration ordered** the **bus companies** to **comply** with **Supreme Court rulings** on the **desegregation** of **buses** and **bus terminals**. The bus companies **agreed** and the **Freedom Rides ended** in **September 1961**.

The Freedom Rides had some Successes

1) The Rides were a **triumph** for **direct action** as they attracted **federal government support** for the **desegregation** of **bus services** in the South. They also showed that **civil rights** groups could **work together successfully**.
2) **CORE** gained a lot of respect for organising the campaign, and **SNCC activists** who **joined** the **Rides increased** the **prestige** of their **organisation**. SNCC **influenced** many **young black people**, especially in the **South**, to join **local campaigns** for **change**.
3) The Rides proved that **Kennedy** would be **more supportive** of the **civil rights movement** than **Eisenhower**.

The Freedom Rides Split Opinions

1) The **Freedom Riders'** use of direct action was **unpopular** with many **African Americans** in the **South**. A large proportion of **young black people** from the **South** had **migrated** to the **North**, leaving the **older generation behind**. These older people were reluctant to support **CORE** and **SNCC** because they felt that these organisations **stirred up trouble** and then **left**.
2) The Rides and direct action were **condemned** by many **newspapers** and people of all races because they **provoked violence**. However, most people, including **newspapers** in **Alabama**, **condemned** the **violence** of **white racists**.
3) The strength of **white opposition** to the **Rides** in the **South** was **evident** from the **violence** that was inflicted on the **Riders**. Organisations such as the **Citizens' Councils of America** claimed that the **Freedom Riders** were **communist agents** working to **undermine US society**.
4) King tried to get **CORE**, the **SCLC** and **SNCC** to **work together** on the **Rides** to **create publicity**, but **King's critics** claimed that he was trying to **hijack** the **Rides** to **promote himself** and the **SCLC**. **CORE demanded** that the **SCLC** should **publicly recognise** that it was **CORE** who had **started** the **Rides**.

The Albany Movement

The civil rights movement wasn't always successful in the 1960s. Activists struggled to make an impact in Albany, Georgia, where the police chief developed his own tactics to deal with peaceful protesters. Back to the drawing board.

The **Albany Movement** wanted an **End** to **Segregation**

1) Following the success of the **Greensboro sit-ins** and the **Freedom Rides**, **SNCC** decided to **challenge discrimination** in **Albany**, **Georgia.** This was known as the **Albany Movement** and it lasted from 1961 to 1962.
2) In November 1961 **SNCC** members organised **sit-ins** in **segregated facilities** in **Albany**, such as **bus stations** which were **still segregated** despite the **Supreme Court's ruling** (Boynton v Virginia). **Boycotts** were also used to **put pressure** on the **city's authorities**, but they **refused** to **compromise**.
3) In **December**, **King** went to Albany and became **heavily involved** in the **protests** there. **Some SNCC leaders** had **criticised King** for showing **poor leadership** during the **Freedom Rides** — and they now felt that King was trying to **impose** his leadership on a **local movement**.
4) King's arrival **failed** to help the **Albany Movement** make any **progress**. **Albany's police chief**, **Laurie Pritchett**, had **studied King's protest methods** and had **developed** a **strategy** which would **neutralise** them.

- **Pritchett arrested** a **large number** of **demonstrators** but **made sure** that **none** of his **police officers mistreated** them in public.
- In **July 1962 King** was given a **jail sentence**, but was **soon released** after **Pritchett arranged** for his **fine** to be **paid**.
- **Pritchett's restraint** meant that the **federal government** had **no need** to **intervene** and the **press lost interest** in the campaign.

5) After a **year** of **protests**, the **Albany Movement** had largely ended in **failure**. The interstate bus facilities were **desegregated**, but instead of integrating its facilities the city **sold off** its **swimming pool** and **closed** all its **parks.** Albany's city officials also **refused** to **desegregate** its **schools**.

Many civil rights activists **Questioned King's Leadership**

The **failure** of the **Albany Movement** led to **divisions** between the **different civil rights organisations**.

1) **SNCC** became **increasingly disillusioned** with **King's methods** of **peaceful protest**, and began to consider using more **violent tactics** to **achieve their aims**. Albany proved that peaceful protests **didn't** always work.
2) **King** was also **criticised** for **not uniting** the efforts of **SNCC** and **SCLC** to ensure that they worked **together effectively**.
3) The **NAACP** wanted **no part** in the **Albany Movement** as they saw it as **confrontational**. The NAACP **didn't like** the **SCLC** and **SNCC's tactics** and they **resented** the fact that **King** wanted them to **cover** his **legal expenses**.
4) However, **King learnt** from the Albany Movement's **failure**. He was **convinced** that it had **failed** because the protesters **hadn't** singled out **one** or **two targets** to **concentrate on** — instead they **demonstrated against segregation** as a **whole**. He also believed that the **best way** to get **political change** was to **boycott white businesses**, so that **white businessmen** would **demand action**.

Practice Questions

Q1 What were the Freedom Rides?

Q2 Why did some African Americans resent the Freedom Rides?

Q3 What were the achievements of the Freedom Rides?

Q4 Give two reasons why the Albany Movement failed.

The Freedom Rides — not the bus home from school...

The Freedom Rides and the Albany Movement were important tests for the policy of direct action. These campaigns highlighted some of the flaws in direct action, and they provided several lessons for King on how to organise direct action effectively.

Martin Luther King, Jr.

Martin Luther King, Jr., was the most influential figure of this period — so you should know a bit about who he was, where he came from and what the major influences on his civil rights activism were.

King came from a Middle-Class Family

1) **King** was **born** in **1929** in **Atlanta, Georgia**. King's **father** was a **Baptist minister** and an **NAACP activist**.
2) King grew up in a **segregated society** and went to **black schools**. King **claimed** that he became aware of the **issue** of **race** when a **white friend** told him that they **couldn't** play together because he was '**coloured**'.
3) King studied sociology at **Morehouse College** in **Atlanta**. During his **final year** at **Morehouse** he was **ordained** as a **Baptist minister** by his father. King continued his studies at a **theological seminary** in **Pennsylvania** before going on to do a **doctorate** at **Boston University's School of Theology**.
4) In **1953** King **married Coretta Scott** and in **1954** they moved to **Montgomery**, **Alabama**.

King's Philosophy had Several Influences

King was **heavily influenced** by his **Christian faith**.

1) King's father had **very conservative** religious beliefs and King **didn't agree** with his **father's literal interpretation** of the **Bible**. As a result, King was **initially against** a **career** in the **church**.
2) However, King retained his **strong religious beliefs**, and while at Morehouse College he realised that **religion** could have a **social purpose**, and that as a **minister** he could **fight against injustice**. The **black church** was the **heart** of many **black communities**, especially in the **South**, and the **preachers** were often **community leaders**. As a Baptist minister, King was able to play a **crucial role** in **organising** civil rights campaigns.
3) King's **background** as a **preacher** also helped him to **speak passionately** and **persuasively**, so that he could **communicate** his **philosophy** to **ordinary people**.
4) **King's Christian beliefs** can be seen in his **ideology** of **love** and **forgiveness**. King wanted a **peaceful solution** to the problems in society. He didn't want to use **violence** and **hate**.

King was also inspired by the leader of the **Indian independence movement**, **Mohandas Gandhi** (1869-1948). King said that while **Jesus** provided his **movement** with its **goals**, it was **Gandhi** who provided it with its **tactics**.

1) **Gandhi** was opposed to **British colonial rule** in **India** and hoped to gain **India's independence**. Gandhi used **boycotts**, **non-violent protest** and **civil disobedience** (rebelling against **unjust** laws) to oppose the British.
2) Gandhi's **tactics** were very **effective** and they proved that people could **oppose injustice without** resorting to **violence**. Gandhi's actions received a lot of **international coverage** and **brought worldwide attention** to his **campaign** — this greatly **embarrassed** the **British**.

King recognised the Importance of Direct Action

1) As a **minister** in **Montgomery**, King **persuaded** his **congregation** to **register** to **vote** and to **join** the **NAACP**. However, as a **key member** of the **Montgomery Bus Boycott** (see p.15), King saw the **power** of **direct action**. King also learned from **Greensboro** (see p.17) and the **Freedom Rides** (see p.18) that **civil disobedience** and a **confrontational approach** attracted **media attention** and **federal assistance**.
2) **King** used a **mixture** of these **tactics** in the **campaigns** he led. In **Birmingham** (see p.22), King **provoked confrontations** (even **controversially** using **children** in the later marches) with the city's **brutal police force**.
3) King knew that if the police **attacked peaceful marches** it would lead to **national** and **international media coverage** of his campaigns and **expose** the **brutality** and **injustices** of **white supremacists**.
4) King gained federal support for his actions by using the **threat** of his leadership being **replaced** by that of more **militant black activists**, like **Malcolm X** (see p.27). **Robert Kennedy**, **US Attorney General**, pointed out that the Kennedy administration **needed** to **support King** otherwise "**worse leaders**" could take his place.

Martin Luther King, Jr.

King was an influential figure in many of the civil rights campaigns, but you should remember that he wasn't always successful and that he received a lot of criticism from other civil rights campaigners.

*King played a **Key Role** in a lot of civil rights **Campaigns***

1) King led several campaigns — in **April 1963** he launched the **successful Birmingham Campaign** (see p.22) and in **August 1963** helped lead the **March on Washington** (see p.23), where he gave his **'I Have a Dream' speech**. King also organised the 1966 **Chicago Campaign** (see p.25). His last campaign, in **1968**, was **against poverty** (see p.25).
2) King played a major role in the 1955 **Montgomery Bus Boycott** as president of **MIA** (see p.15), which **propelled him** to the **forefront** of the civil rights movement. King **joined forces** with **SNCC** in the **1965 Selma Campaign** (see p.24) and again in **1966** for **James Meredith's March Against Fear** (see p.30).
3) King was a **latecomer** to the **campaign** of **sit-ins** sparked off by the **Greensboro sit-ins** (see p.17) in **February 1960**, but he urged the students to **create SNCC** to **organise** their **campaigns**. In **December 1961**, King also **joined** the **Albany Movement** (see p.19) **after** it had **begun**, and he ended up **leading** the **protests** there.
4) In **1961** King gave his **support** to **CORE's Freedom Rides** (see p.18), but **refused** to become a **Rider** himself. He played **no part** in **SNCC's Mississippi Freedom Summer** in **1964**, although he did voice his support (see p.24).

King had a **massive impact** on the **civil rights movement**. He was a **popular** and **unifying leader** who **appealed** to **both African Americans** and **white people**. **No later leader** of the **civil rights movement** had such broad **influence** and **popularity**.

King** attracted a lot of **Criticism

King was attacked by more **radical** civil rights groups such as **SNCC** for being **too moderate** and **too willing** to work with **white people**. The more moderate **NAACP** felt King was **too radical** and **endangered** the **civil rights movement**.

1) King's **tactics**, such as using **children** in the **Birmingham Campaign** (see p.22), were **condemned** by some for being too **confrontational** and **provoking violence**.
2) In **1967** King spoke out **against** the **Vietnam War** (see p.29) which made him **very unpopular** with the **majority** of **Americans** at that time. King was **criticised** by the **NAACP**, because his views made it **more difficult** for **President Johnson** to **support** the **civil rights movement**.
3) King's **popularity** and **publicity-courting** led to **attacks** on his **personality**. Moderates and radicals claimed that King was **arrogant** and **self-promoting**, and that he **hijacked** other people's **campaigns**.
4) When King **failed** to **act** he was also **criticised**. **SNCC** members were **disillusioned** by **King's refusal** to join the **Freedom Rides** (see p.18). When **King** was asked to **participate** in the **Rides** he replied that he'd choose where and when he'd face his "**Golgotha**" — a reference to the **place** where **Jesus died**. As a result of **King comparing** himself to **Jesus**, some **SNCC** members **mockingly** dubbed him '**De Lawd**'.

The **Federal Bureau of Investigation (FBI)** believed that King was a **subversive influence** on **America**, and that he had **links** to **communism**. The FBI **bugged** King's **phones** and **spied** on him to try to find **evidence** which they could use to **discredit** him and **undermine** his **leadership**. The FBI learnt that King had **many affairs**, and in **1964** they sent **King** and his **wife letters** threatening to **expose** him. The FBI **monitored King** until his **assassination** in **1968**.

Practice Questions

Q1 Name two influences on King's philosophy.

Q2 Why did King attract a lot of criticism from civil rights groups?

Glossary

FBI — the Federal Bureau of Investigation is a federal police organisation which investigates serious crimes and threats to national security.

black church — churches run and attended by African Americans.

MLK — the Philosopher King...

King was portrayed as a hero, and it was hard for him to live up to his idealised image. King had his flaws, and received a lot of criticism, but his charisma, courage and non-violent philosophy were crucial to the success of the struggle for civil rights in America.

King's Campaigns

It was in Birmingham, Alabama, in 1963, that the civil rights movement scored one of its most important victories. King proved that he'd learnt from the mistakes made in Albany by leading an effective campaign of peaceful protests.

Birmingham, Alabama, was the Next Battleground for Civil Rights

King and the **SCLC** learnt several **important lessons** from the **Albany Movement** (see p.19). King knew that a **violent response** to a **peaceful protest** would bring a lot of **publicity**, and **possibly** the **intervention** of the **federal government**.

1) King chose **Birmingham**, **Alabama**, as the SCLC's next target for protest for **many reasons**:

- **Birmingham** was **rigidly segregated** and African Americans experienced **severe discrimination** there.
- The **NAACP** had been **banned** in **Alabama** in **1956**.
- **Eugene 'Bull' Connor**, the man in charge of **Birmingham's police**, had **close links** to the **Ku Klux Klan**. Connor let the Klan **operate freely** in the **city** and he had **allowed** them to **attack** the **Freedom Riders** in **1961** (see page 18).
- **King** was **confident** that **Connor** and his **police force** would **overreact** to any **demonstrations** in the city, which would draw **media coverage** to the **campaign**.

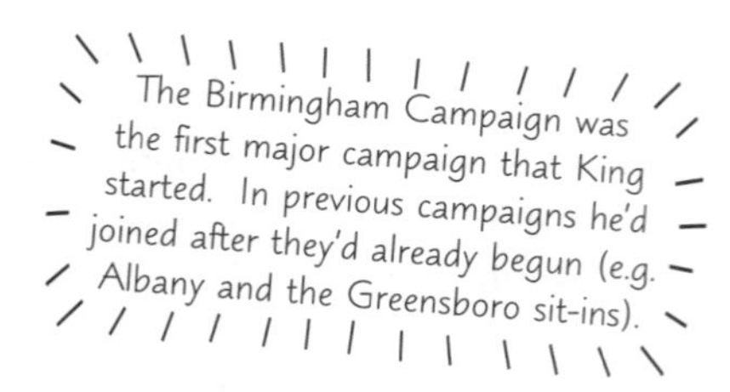

2) Unlike in Albany, King targeted **segregation** in **public spaces** — such as the city's **major shopping areas**, **administrative buildings**, **schools** and **parks**. King hoped to **put pressure** on **local businesses** through **boycotts**, so that **business leaders** would **force** the **city's authorities** to **give in to** King's **demands**.
3) Birmingham was seen as an **important test** because many felt that if **segregation** could be **stopped** in **Birmingham**, then it could be **stopped anywhere** in the **South**.

The police used Violence against the Protesters

1) The **Birmingham Campaign** began in **April 1963**. **King** was soon **arrested** and **jailed**, but he **refused** to be **bailed** because he knew his **imprisonment** would help bring **national** and **international media attention** to the situation.
2) In prison, **King wrote** his **'Letter from Birmingham Jail'** in which he **explained** his **philosophy** and **argued** that **civil rights campaigners** had to take **direct action** instead of **waiting** for **change** to happen.
3) The **first month** of the campaign was **relatively peaceful**. **Connor didn't** use **excessive violence** against the protesters, and **few African Americans** were **prepared** to be **arrested**.
4) However, the campaign **changed dramatically** in **May**. The **SCLC** were **struggling** to **find recruits** for their campaign, so they called on **thousands** of **school children** and **students** to take part in demonstrations. This was a **highly controversial** move and was **criticised** by both **Thurgood Marshall** and **Malcolm X** (see p.27).
5) **Connor responded** by using **police dogs** and **powerful fire hoses** to **disperse** the **demonstrators**, and the **jails** were **filled** with **over a thousand children** — some as young as **six years old**.
6) The **images** of protestors being **attacked** by **dogs** or being **pinned** to **walls** by **fire hoses** were **shown** on **television** in the **US** and around the **world**. The **Soviet Union highlighted** the **violence** in their **radio broadcasts**. **Bull Connor** had delivered a **huge propaganda victory** to the **civil rights campaign**.

The Campaign was a Success

1) The **SCLC** reached an **agreement** with the **city's authorities** for **widespread desegregation** in **Birmingham** and an **end** to **discrimination** in **employment**.
2) **Some** of these **promises weren't kept**, but **most shops** and **public places** were made **open** to **all people**, **regardless** of **colour**.
3) The **Birmingham campaign** was a **huge success** for **King**. He became **recognised nationally** and **internationally** as the **leader** of the **civil rights movement** in the US. It also **pushed President Kennedy** to **propose** a **Civil Rights Bill** to **Congress** (see p.23).

King's Campaigns

A defining moment of the civil rights campaign was when Martin Luther King gave his famous 'I Have a Dream' speech to thousands of people in Washington, D.C., in August 1963. I had the exact same dream, except mine was about bears.

King Played a Leading Role in the March on Washington in 1963

1) **Civil rights campaigners** were **boosted** by King's **success** in **Birmingham** (see p.22) and the main civil rights organisations (**CORE**, **SNCC**, the **SCLC** and the **NAACP**) **united** for the **March on Washington for Jobs and Freedom**.
2) On **28th August 1963** around **250 000** people (including **60 000 white people**) peacefully **listened** to **speeches** by **civil rights leaders**. **King delivered** his most **memorable speech** of all — **'I Have a Dream'** — which was **broadcast** across the **US** and the **world**. The speech called for **civil rights** and **peaceful integration** and **cooperation** between **black** and **white people**.
3) Although the **March on Washington** was **criticised** by the **Black Power leader Malcolm X** (see p.27) as a **"picnic"** and a **"farce"**, the event showed that different **civil rights organisations** could **work together** for the **same aims** — **political freedom** and **better economic conditions** for **African Americans**.

© Everett Collection/Rex Features

Martin Luther King addressing a huge audience in Washington, D.C., 1963.

Some Civil Rights Legislation was Passed by Congress Before 1964

Two Civil Rights Acts were passed in **Eisenhower's second term** as **president**, but they weren't **very effective**.

- The **1957 Civil Rights Act** was **intended** to **guarantee** the **right** of African Americans to **vote unhindered**, but its powers were **weakened** by **amendments** to the bill passed by **pro-segregationists** in **Congress**.
- The **1960 Civil Rights Act** gave African Americans the right to **challenge discrimination** carried out by **voter registrars**. However, this process required the **cooperation** of **Southern courts** and **officials**, who were usually **opposed** to **civil rights**. Consequently the **number** of **registered black voters** in the South **barely increased**.

Congress Passed a Civil Rights Act in 1964

A bill becomes an act (a law) when it passed by Congress and approved by the president.

1) In **1963**, after the **pressure** caused by **King's Birmingham Campaign** and the **March on Washington**, **President Kennedy** began putting together a **Civil Rights Bill**. However, it **stalled** in **Congress** when **Kennedy** was **assassinated** in **November 1963**.
2) **Kennedy's successor** was **Lyndon Johnson**. **Johnson** was **committed** to **passing Kennedy's Civil Rights Bill**, and used **Kennedy's popularity** to **promote** it. Johnson claimed the bill was a **powerful memorial** to the **dead president** and should be passed in Kennedy's honour.
3) After a **long** and **bitter battle** in **Congress** the **bill** was **signed into law** on **2nd July 1964**.

The **main points** of the **Civil Rights Act** were:

1) **All segregation** was **outlawed**.
2) Action was to be taken to **enforce** the **integration** of the **entire education system**.
3) **Discrimination** in **employment** due to **race** (or **gender**) was **forbidden**.
4) But **voter registration tests** used to **bar** black voters **weren't banned**.

Practice Questions

Q1 Why did King choose Birmingham, Alabama, for a civil rights campaign?

Q2 How did President Kennedy's assassination help the passing of the Civil Rights Bill?

Exam Question

Q1 How important was Martin Luther King's contribution to the civil rights movement in the years 1955-1963? [30 Marks]

MLK in Washington — The King's Speech...

Kennedy had initially been reluctant to support civil rights because many members of his party were Southerners. The Birmingham Campaign and the March on Washington helped to convince him to draw up a Civil Rights Bill, which Johnson later passed.

The Freedom Summer and Selma

The 1964 Civil Rights Act had one big flaw — it didn't outlaw restrictions on voting. African Americans continued to be prevented from voting in the South, and one of the worst states was Mississippi. SNCC went there to try to help out.

The *Freedom Summer* was a *Voter Registration Drive* in *Mississippi*

1) In **1964 SNCC** organised the **Freedom Summer** campaign in **Mississippi** to try to **increase voter registration**.
2) In Mississippi **less than 7%** of **eligible African Americans** were **registered** to **vote**. Approximately **1000 volunteers** from the **North** came to the state to run **Freedom Schools**, with **classes** on **politics** and **health education**, and to take African Americans to **voter registration offices**.
3) Most of the **white people** of **Mississippi** were **hostile** to the **Freedom Summer**. **Volunteers** were **attacked** and their **homes** were **bombed**. **Three civil rights activists**, **two** of whom were **white**, were **murdered** by the **Ku Klux Klan**. The incident brought a great deal of **media attention** to the **Freedom Summer**.
4) **Despite** all their **activities**, **SNCC failed** to **register** many **black voters**, due to **opposition** from the **police** and the **Klan**. The **fierce resistance** which **SNCC** faced **convinced** many **members** that **non-violent methods** of opposition **weren't working** and a more **militant** approach was **needed**.

1964 was a **presidential election year**, but **Mississippi's Democratic Party refused** to allow **African Americans** to **vote** in their **primary election**. Activists formed the **Mississippi Freedom Democratic Party** (**MFDP**) and held their own **primary election**. The MFDP **sent delegates** to the **Democratic Party's national convention**, but the delegates were only offered **two seats** at the convention and told that they **couldn't vote**. The MFDP **rejected** the offer and **protested** against their unfair treatment.

The *Civil Rights Movement* went to *Selma, Alabama*, in *1965*

1) The SCLC had **struggled** to achieve much since the **Birmingham Campaign**, but they saw **Selma, Alabama**, as the **perfect place** to launch a **non-violent campaign** against **segregation** and **discrimination**.
2) King chose Selma because **less** than **2%** of the town's **African Americans** of **voting age** were **registered** to **vote**. The town's authorities had also **ignored** Johnson's **Civil Rights Act** and **continued segregating** African Americans, and the police chief, **Sheriff Jim Clark**, was determined to **uphold** all aspects of **segregation**, by **force** if necessary.
3) **King's SCLC** and **SNCC joined forces** to demand reforms in **Selma**. King and the SCLC believed that **Sheriff Jim Clark** would **react violently** to any **protest** in the town and create the **publicity** needed to ensure that a **Voting Rights Act** was **passed** by **Congress**.
4) **Jim Clark's police** responded with **brutality** to demonstrations organised by the SCLC and SNCC, and he **personally attacked** a **black woman**. On another occasion a **young African American**, Jimmie Lee Jackson, was **killed** while trying to **protect** his **mother** from being **beaten** by the **police**.
5) However, after **failing** to **generate** much **media attention** the **SCLC** and **SNCC** decided to go on a **peaceful march** from **Selma** to **Montgomery** (fifty miles away), to **commemorate** the **tenth anniversary** of the **Montgomery Bus Boycott** and to promote the need for a **Voting Rights Act**.
6) **Two attempts** to stage the march **ended just outside Selma**, with **state troopers beating** the **marchers** and using **tear gas**. A **third attempt** was **protected** by **federal troops** and the **FBI**, and was **peacefully completed** by **25 000** people.

Congress Passed the *Voting Rights Act* in *1965*

The **violence** in **Selma** and the **bravery** of **SNCC** and **SCLC activists** persuaded **President Johnson** to **reconsider** the **major flaw** in the **1964 Civil Rights Act** — **not addressing** the **restrictions** on a **person's right** to **vote**.

1) **President Johnson** responded to the Selma campaign by **pushing** the **Voting Rights Act** through **Congress**. **All restrictions** on **registration** and **voting** were **banned** — including **literacy tests**. **Federal authorities** were given the power to **make sure** that the **law** was **obeyed**.
2) The **Voting Rights Act** was a **triumph** for the **civil rights movement**, and marked a step towards **ensuring** the **political equality** of **all races** in the **US**.
3) However, while the **Voting Rights Act** ensured that **African Americans** had **de jure rights**, the **de facto situation** in America was still one where **discrimination** and **inequality** were **widespread**.

King's Later Campaigns

The civil rights acts passed between 1957 and 1965 ensured that all races would, in theory, be given equal treatment. But African Americans and other ethnic minorities remained disadvantaged in many ways.

By 1968 African Americans had De Jure Civil Rights

1) The **1965 Voting Rights Act** led to a **large increase** in the number of **black voters**.
2) The **majority** of **black children** in the **South** still went to **segregated schools** in **1968**, but the numbers were **declining**. **African Americans** had more chance of going **university** in **1968** than **ever before**.
3) The **segregation** of **facilities**, **buses** and **public places** was coming to an **end**. In some cases **local authorities closed facilities** to **avoid desegregation**, but **hundreds** of **Southern cities** were **desegregated** by **1968**.
4) However, African Americans were still **economically disadvantaged**. Most **African Americans** still worked in **low-skilled** and **low-paid jobs**. In the North, many African Americans lived in **ghettos** (see p.28) — this created **de facto segregation** in other areas such as **education**.
5) The US remained a **divided nation** — in 1968 the **pro-segregationist George Wallace** ran for president as an **American Independent**. In **five states** in the **South** he won **more votes** than the **Democrats** or the **Republicans**.

King went to Chicago to Campaign for Economic and Social Equality

1) **King** chose **Chicago** to **highlight** the **problem** of **economic** and **social inequality** in the **North** because the city had a **large**, **oppressed black community**. King's campaign, which was his **first** in the **North**, began in **June 1966**.
2) Chicago was **dominated** by the **Democratic Party**, under the **leadership** of **Mayor Richard Daley**. **Daley** had a **firm grip** on the city, but was **unwilling** to take **positive action** to ease **racial discrimination** in areas such as **housing**.
3) **King** used **methods** which had **worked** in the **South** — he organised **marches** through **white neighbourhoods** to **provoke** a **reaction**. At one march **King** and his **followers** were attacked by an **angry mob** of **white men** and King commented that they were **more vicious** than anything he'd experienced in the **South**.
4) King's marches **forced Mayor Daley** to **negotiate**, but Daley **never carried out** his **vague promises** of **reform**, and he made further **marches illegal**.
5) King's campaign **failed** because it was **unfocused**. King made **demands** for **economic** and **social change** which **couldn't** happen **overnight** and required **massive federal funding**. The **sheer size** of the **black population** in **Chicago**, which was **around one million**, also **presented big problems** for **King** because it was **hard** to **organise** so many people.
6) King also struggled because **African Americans** in **Chicago weren't** as **strongly influenced** by **Christian ministers** as in the **South**. King's **methods** were seen as **irrelevant**, and **Northern African Americans** became **interested** in the new **Black Power movement** instead.

King's Last Campaign was against Poverty

1) **King's next campaign** centred on a **gathering** of **poor people** in **Washington, D.C.**, in **1968**. The aim of King's **'Poor People's Campaign'** was to create a **coalition** of the **poor** of **all races** to **demand laws** to **combat poverty**.
2) However, on **4th April 1968**, **King** was **assassinated** in **Memphis, Tennessee**. The **demonstration** in **Washington took place** in his **memory** in **May**, but it **fell apart** without King's leadership.
3) **One week** after King's assassination **President Johnson signed** into **law** the **1968 Civil Rights (Fair Housing) Act**, which **prohibited racial discrimination** in the **sale**, **rental** and **mortgaging** of **housing**. However, the act **didn't** provide the government with the **power** to **enforce** this **new law**, so it **wasn't** very **effective**.

Practice Question

Exam Question

Q1 How successful was the civil rights movement in securing equality for African Americans by 1968? [30 Marks]

King's death was followed by riots — not really what he would've wanted...

Martin Luther King's death was a big blow to those campaigning for equality in America, and many African Americans reacted with violence. There were riots in over 100 cities across America, which resulted in many deaths and millions of dollars worth of damage.

Introduction to Section 3

Oh boy — it's my favourite page. Look at all those dates, important people and historical terms for you to learn. Yay!

Here's a **Quick Summary** of **Section Three**

This section deals with **Malcolm X**, **Black Power** and the **Black Panthers**. Here's some useful information:

- **Malcolm X** was an **important influence** on many African Americans. He became a **religious minister** in the **Nation of Islam**, whose views on **black nationalism** and **separatism inspired** the **Black Power movement.**
- There were **hundreds** of **race riots** during the **1960s**, the **worst** of which were the **Harlem Riot** in **1964**, the **Watts Riots** in **1965** and the **Newark** and **Detroit Riots** in **1967**.
- **Stokely Carmichael** became **SNCC's Chairman** in **1966** and he launched the **'Black Power' slogan** in **June** that year. Carmichael **radicalised SNCC** — he **expelled** its **white members**, and focused on **black nationalism.**
- In 1966 **Huey Newton** and **Bobby Seale** created the **Black Panthers** — a militant **African-American organisation** which promoted **black nationalism**. They also developed **programmes** to **help black communities.**

Learn the **Key Dates** of the **Black Power Movement**

- **Malcolm X assassinated.**
- **Watts Riots.**

- **March Against Fear** — **'Black Power'** slogan popularised by **Stokely Carmichael.**
- **Black Panthers formed.**

- **Newark Riots.**
- **Detroit Riots.**

Malcolm X

Important People in this Period:

- **Malcolm X** — A black nationalist and Nation of Islam minister.
- **Elijah Muhammad** — Head of the Nation of Islam from 1934-1975.
- **Stokely Carmichael** — Chairman of SNCC from 1966-1967.
- **Floyd McKissick** — Head of CORE from 1966-1968.
- **Huey Newton & Bobby Seale** — Cofounders of the Black Panthers.

Make sure you know what these **Historical Terms** mean

- **Nation of Islam** — A religious black nationalist group which wanted to create a separate state in the US for African Americans.
- **Black Power** — A slogan popularised by Stokely Carmichael which meant different things to different people, including black nationalism, black separatism, black pride, black violence and black supremacy.
- **Black Nationalism** — The belief that African Americans should govern themselves.
- **Black Separatism** — The belief that African Americans should reject integration and live separately from white people.
- **Black Panthers** — A militant African-American organisation inspired by Black Power, Marxism and black nationalism. Its members were prepared to use violence to achieve their aims.

Malcolm X

Malcolm X was an interesting figure in this period, and his ideas had a lasting influence on the civil rights movement — especially on Black Power. So that's why he's got a page all to himself.

Malcolm X came from a Poor Background

1) **Malcolm Little** was **born** in **1925** into a **large**, **poor family** in **Nebraska**. His **father** died when Malcolm was **six years old** — Malcolm later claimed that his father was **murdered** by racists. When Malcolm was **fourteen** his **mother** was committed to a **psychiatric hospital**, so he was sent to live with his sister in Boston.
2) Malcolm became involved in petty crime, and in **1946** he was **imprisoned** for **burglary**. In prison he **read widely** and found a **new purpose** in **life** when he **joined** the **Nation of Islam**.
3) Malcolm **dropped** his **surname**, **Little**, which he regarded as his **slave name** (given to his **slave ancestors** by their **owner**). Instead he chose **'X'**, which **symbolised** his lost African tribal name.

Malcolm was influenced by the Nation Of Islam

1) While in prison **Malcolm joined** the **Nation of Islam** (**NOI**), a small **black separatist** organisation which was **inspired** by **Islam**, but which had its **own beliefs** and **practices**. It was led by **Elijah Muhammad**.
2) The NOI were **black supremacists**, believing that **their race** was **superior** and that **white people** were "**devils**" who had been **created** by an **evil black scientist**. The NOI thought **black people** should **live separately** from **white people**.
3) The **NOI** required **complete loyalty** and **self-discipline** from its members. **Drugs**, **tobacco** and **alcohol** were **forbidden**, and members were encouraged to have **pride** in their **race** and in **themselves**.
4) When Malcolm was **released** from prison in **1952** he became a **minister** in the **NOI** and **attracted attention** as an **influential** and **charismatic speaker**. He gained a **national audience** through **appearances** on **radio** and **television**.
5) However, Malcolm later became **disillusioned** with the **NOI**. In **1963** he learned that **Elijah Muhammad**, who preached **sexual morality**, was having several **affairs**. Malcolm also became **frustrated** that the **NOI hadn't joined** the **civil rights struggle**. He **left** the **NOI** in **1964** and **converted** to **Sunni Islam**.
6) In **February 1965 Malcolm** was **murdered** in **New York** by members of the **NOI**.

Malcolm's Philosophy was Different to King's

1) Malcolm X's **upbringing** meant he could **identify** with **poor African Americans** in the **North** and **understand** their **anger**. Malcolm's **powerful rhetoric** on **black nationalism** seemed to suggest a **solution** to the **injustices** that **poor**, **angry African Americans** faced, and it formed the basis of the **Black Power movement** (see p.30).
2) **Malcolm** was **critical** of **King's philosophy**. King wanted to end racial discrimination **peacefully** and **integrate white** and **black people**. In contrast, **Malcolm agreed** with **Elijah Muhammad's** view that the **races** should be **kept separate**. He also disliked **King's peaceful protests**, because he felt that **African Americans** were entitled to **fight** for their rights against **white racists** and use violence **if necessary**.
3) He also believed that **African Americans** should **control** the **economy** in their **own communities**, and **shouldn't** use **white people's businesses**. By becoming **economically self-sufficient**, African Americans would no longer be **dependent** on **white people**.

- However, **Malcolm's views** began to **change significantly** after he **left** the **NOI**, and in particular when he made a **pilgrimage** to **Mecca** in **1964**. He **realised** that **Islam embraced people** of **all races** and **didn't** discriminate. He also accepted that some **white people** worked **tirelessly** to **help black people**.
- Malcolm began to **edge towards** the **mainstream ideas** of the **civil rights movement**. However, he continued to believe in the use of **violence** against **racism**.

Practice Question

Q1 How did Malcolm X's views on civil rights change during his life?

Malcolm X — no one knows what happened to Malcolms I to IX...

Malcolm once claimed his role was "to remind the white man of the alternative to Dr. King". Malcolm knew that white liberals feared his militant black nationalism, which made them more willing to work with King to prevent African Americans turning to violence.

Discrimination in the North

Things were different in the North compared to the South, but there was still a lot of economic and social discrimination against African Americans. In the 1960s, tensions in the North would boil over into violence.

The **Black Population** in the **North Grew Rapidly**

1) Throughout most of the 20th century, **conditions** for **African Americans** were better in the North than in the **South**, because there was **less segregation**, **jobs** were **better paid**, and there was **freedom** to **vote**. As a result, **millions** of African Americans **migrated north**.
2) **Unlike** in the **South**, where the **black population** was **spread across** each **state**, African Americans in the **North** were **concentrated** in **large towns** and **cities**. Between **1940** and **1965**, the black population **rose rapidly** in **Northern cities** like **Chicago** and **Detroit**.
3) The **growth** in the **urban black population** in the **North** and the practice of **segregation** in **housing** led to the **creation** of **ghettos** — **poor all-black** areas of a **city**.
4) Although **segregation** in the **North** was **not as bad** as it was in the **South**, African Americans still experienced a lot of **prejudice** and **discrimination** from the **white community**.

President Johnson hoped to address some of the **inequalities** facing **African Americans** with his **'Great Society' programme**. It was aimed at **helping** the **poorest members** of **US society**, but the **programme** was **undermined** — much of its **funding** was **cut** due to **increased spending** on the **Vietnam War**.

African Americans in the **North** suffered **De Facto Segregation** at **Work**

1) **Very few** African Americans in the North managed to get **skilled jobs** or **managerial positions**. As in the South, they mainly ended up as **poorly paid**, **unskilled** labourers — but even this manual labour was becoming **scarce** because of the **increasing** use of **machinery** in **factories**.
2) Although many black men were **trained** to work in **construction**, e.g. as **plumbers** and **electricians**, they **couldn't** get **work** because they needed to be **members** of **trade unions**, and many unions **refused** them **membership**.
3) It was also hard for African Americans in the North to **improve** their **prospects** because **schools** in the **ghettos** were **underfunded**. State schools **received funding** from **local taxes**, but the money gained from the taxes was **reduced** because **middle-class white people left** the **cities** to live in **suburbs** — a process known as **'white flight'** (see below).
4) The **rate** of **unemployment** for **African Americans** was around **twice** that of **white Americans** during the **1960s**.

De Facto Segregation affected **Housing**

1) The government began a **highway building programme** in the **1950s**. This led to the building of **suburbs** around the major cities. However, it was usually **only white people** who could **afford** houses in the **suburbs**. This led to **'white flight'**, where white people **left** the **cities**.
2) **African Americans** were often **prevented** from **living** in the **suburbs** — some houses were **specifically not** for sale to "members of **other than** the **Caucasian race**". In **1970**, America's **suburban population** was **95% white**.
3) **Poverty**, **poor education** and **unemployment** meant that African Americans struggled to **escape** the ghettos.

Discrimination in the **North** led to **Race Riots**

1) **Resentment** in the **ghettos** across America led to over **two hundred race riots** between **1964** and **1968**.
2) The riots were often **triggered** by incidents of **police brutality**. They **resulted** in **dozens** of people being **killed**, **millions** of **dollars** worth of **damage**, and in some cases the use of **soldiers** to **quell** the **riots**.
3) The **highest profile** riot was in **Detroit** in **1967**. A **police raid** on an **unlicensed bar** led to a huge riot which lasted for **five days** and left **43 people dead**. President Johnson had to deploy **thousands** of **soldiers** to **subdue** the **rioters**.
4) In 1965 a riot in **Watts**, **Los Angeles**, began after police arrested an African American man for drink driving and it led to **34 deaths**. **26** people **died** in the **1967 riot** in **Newark**, **New Jersey**, which was triggered by a **rumours** of **police brutality** against a **black taxi-driver**.

Splits in the Civil Rights Movement

Tensions always existed between the civil rights organisations, because they had different goals and different methods. All the civil rights groups were competing for attention and financial support — clashes were inevitable.

The **Civil Rights Organisations Divided** for **Several Reasons**

1) **Civil rights organisations** disagreed over a **number** of **key issues**:
   - The **tactics** used to **fight** for **civil rights** — **legal tactics, non-violent direct action,** or **violence**.
   - Whether **black** and **white people** should **work together** in the **same organisations**.
   - Whether **black people** should be **integrated** into **American society**.
2) **SNCC** and the **SCLC** both formed due to **frustration** with the **NAACP's legal challenges**, which many felt were **too slow**. **SNCC** and the **SCLC** were **initially** quite **similar** — both had **white** and **black members** and advocated **non-violent protest** and **civil disobedience**.
3) However, there was growing **disillusionment** with **King's non-violent tactics**. **SNCC** and **CORE**, which were **heavily influenced** by **Malcolm X**, became increasingly **radical** and **militant** as they **promoted black nationalism** and **self-defence** as ways of **achieving civil rights**.
4) Consequently, the **civil rights organisations** fell into **three camps** — **moderates** like the **NAACP**, **radicals** such as **SNCC** and **CORE**, and those groups that lay somewhere between and were **criticised** from **both sides**, such as **King's SCLC**.

The **Vietnam War** widened the **Splits** in the **Civil Rights Movement**

In **1965** President Johnson **increased** the **US's commitment** to Vietnam by deploying **nearly 200 000 combat troops** to **fight communist forces** in the region — it was the start of the major **US military campaign** in **Vietnam**.

1) Many African Americans **opposed** the **Vietnam War**. Opponents argued that the Vietnamese were victims of **white racism**, and that the war had **nothing** to do with **black people**.
2) African Americans also **resented** the fact that while **13%** of **US personnel** in **Vietnam** were **African American**, they comprised about a **quarter** of **military casualties** in **1965**.

A coalition is where several groups with different interests work together towards a common cause.

- The **Vietnam War** contributed to the collapse of the **fragile coalition** of **civil rights organisations**.
- **SNCC** and **CORE strongly opposed** the war and became **increasingly radical** and **militant** in their **anti-war protests**. **Stokely Carmichael** and other members of **SNCC** even visited **communist North Vietnam**.
- After **remaining** quiet on the issue, in **1967 King** eventually spoke out **against** the **war** (see p.21). **King** was **criticised** by the **NAACP** for **harming** the **civil rights** movement as his attack on Johnson's **foreign policy** made it **less likely** that Johnson would support civil rights. **Radicals** attacked King for **not** speaking out **earlier**.
- Despite having **strong reservations** about the war, the NAACP continued to **back Johnson** so that the civil rights movement **wouldn't** be **tarnished** by the **militant anti-war protests**.

3) The **opposition** of **civil rights organisations** to the **Vietnam War** was seen as **unpatriotic** by the **majority** of **Americans**. It also made **Johnson less inclined** to support civil rights, and his **spending** on the **war** diverted **money away** from his **Great Society** programme, which was intended to **tackle inequality**.

Practice Questions

Q1 Give two examples of discrimination against African Americans in the North in this period.

Q2 Describe the effect the Vietnam War had on the relationship between the African-American civil rights organisations.

Break-ups — they're always tough...

The splits that developed in the civil rights movement meant that it began to lose momentum in the late 1960s. The increasing radicalism of parts of the movement cost it support from moderates, and a divided movement meant an end to united campaigns.

Black Power

'Black Power' was a powerful slogan in the 1960s, and it gave African Americans a sense of pride. Black Power appealed to young black people who felt that King's tactics of non-violent protest worked too slowly.

Stokely Carmichael led the Black Power Movement

1) The **Black Power** movement began when **SNCC** and **CORE** developed a more **radical strategy**. They felt the **improvements** in the **legal status** of **African Americans** achieved by **1965** weren't enough, and that there needed to be **major changes** in America's **economy** and **society**. '**Black Power**' became the **slogan** for those who wanted **bigger changes** at a **quicker pace**.
2) **SNCC** and **CORE** underwent a **change of leadership** to reflect this **new ideology**. In **1966 Floyd McKissick** was **elected** as the **head** of **CORE** and **Stokely Carmichael** became **SNCC's chairman**.
3) **McKissick** and **Carmichael** were determined to go in a **radical new direction** — **SNCC** and **CORE** adopted **Malcolm X's** ideas on **black nationalism**, **black separatism** and **self-defence**.
4) In **June 1966 Stokely Carmichael** joined the **March Against Fear** through **Mississippi** to encourage **voter registration**. **Carmichael** used **media coverage** of the march to announce a **new SNCC slogan** — '**Black Power**'.
5) Carmichael **didn't define Black Power**, but it **immediately** became **popular**. For many black people, Black Power **symbolised whatever** they wanted it to **symbolise**. Some saw it as a **demand** for **economic** and **political equality**, others as an affirmation of **black nationalism** and **racial pride**.
6) The **March Against Fear ended** with **King** and his **supporters** chanting '**Freedom Now**' and **Carmichael** and his **supporters** chanting '**Black Power**'. The **division** between the **civil rights organisations** was **very clear**, and **King** admitted that a **total split** was **very close**. The **NAACP refused** to work **alongside SNCC** or the **SCLC**.

James Meredith (see p.16) went on a march through Mississippi to encourage black people to vote, but was shot. While Meredith recovered, civil rights leaders, including King and Carmichael, completed the march.

Black Power had lots of Influences

1) **Malcolm X's confrontational philosophy** and convictions on **black nationalism** and **self-defence** had a **major influence** on the **Black Power movement**. **Malcolm's** own views were **shaped** by his time in the **NOI** (see p.27) and the NOI were in turn **influenced** by **Marcus Garvey** (see p.4), a **black nationalist** and **separatist**. **Garvey** and the **NOI** were **strongly opposed** to **integration** between **black** and **white people** and they felt that **black people** should **create** their **own nation**.
2) The **emphasis** on **violence** in the **Black Power movement** was **influenced** by the **philosopher Frantz Fanon**, who wrote about the **struggle** of **'colonised' people** to **overthrow** their **colonial masters**. **Fanon** believed that the use **violence** to **oppose oppressive regimes** could be **beneficial** to **oppressed people** as it gave them **self-respect**.

Black Power created Divisions in the Civil Rights Movement

1) **SNCC expelled** its white members in **1966**, which marked a **radical change** in their **ideology**. Some SNCC leaders believed that **African Americans** should **determine** their **own destiny** and that the presence of **senior white members** in **SNCC** led to a feeling of **white superiority**.
2) **Carmichael** deepened the **divisions** between the **civil rights organisations** by expressing his views on **how** African Americans should **pursue Black Power**. He argued that **African Americans** had to **work together** to **dominate communities** in which they were in the **majority**, so that they could **serve** their **own interests**.
3) **Moderate civil rights campaigners** argued that true civil rights activists **couldn't** support **Black Power** because it was **opposed** to **integration** and **peaceful cooperation**. King cautioned that **Black Power** gave the impression of **black supremacy**, which would be just as **harmful** as **white supremacy**.
4) **White liberals** who **supported civil rights** disliked **Black Power**, which they saw as **racism** in another form. The link between **Black Power** and **violence** made many Americans **very angry**.

Black Power

SNCC engaged in some community campaigns to help African Americans have a greater say in what happened in the areas where they lived. Ultimately, SNCC's rejection of white people and its radicalism led to its swift downfall.

Black Power had Some Successes

1) Black Power led to an increasing emphasis on the study of **black history** and **culture**. African Americans began to embrace their **African heritage** and some even adopted **African names** — for example, **Carmichael** changed his name to **Kwame Toure**. Others sported **Afro hairstyles** to **draw attention** to their **cultural identity**.
2) Black Power had a **positive psychological** effect on African Americans, giving them **greater self-respect** and **pride**. The terms **'Negro'** and **'colored'** fell **out** of **fashion**, and due to the **popularity** of **Black Power**, **African Americans** started to **refer** to **themselves** as **'black'**.
3) Carmichael believed that **Black Power** required **African Americans** to **control** the **communities** they lived in. In **1965**, **Marion Barry**, the **head** of **SNCC** in **Washington, D.C.**, organised the **'Free D.C. Movement'**. Washington, as the national capital, was **controlled directly** by **Congress**. Barry **campaigned successfully** to give the city, which was **majority African American**, **more say** in its **own affairs**. **Barry** later became **mayor** of **Washington, D.C.**
4) The **Black Panthers** also helped black communities by organising **'survival programmes'** (see p.32) to address some of the **economic**, **medical** and **social problems** facing poor African Americans.

Black Power Damaged SNCC

1) After **SNCC expelled** its **white members** and proclaimed the slogan **'Black Power'**, it scared off **any support** it had from **moderate African Americans** and **white people**. Because Carmichael **never clearly defined** what he meant by **Black Power**, **critics** labelled it a call for **violence**.
2) King was **worried** by **Black Power**, which he called a **"slogan without a programme"** — he **didn't** want African Americans to turn to **hatred** and **violence**. **Roy Wilkins**, the **head** of the **NAACP**, believed that **Black Power** was **racism** in **another form**, **no better** than the **racism** of **white supremacists**. The result of this was that **SNCC lost most** of its **funding** and its **ability** to **function** as an **effective** civil rights organisation. SNCC tried to **ally** with the **Black Panthers**, but it **didn't last**.
3) SNCC's **unrealistic aim** of **black separatism** and its **increasing support** of **violence** caused many people to **distance themselves** from it. SNCC **faded** into **insignificance** and **dissolved altogether** in the **1970s**.

The Media's Portrayal of African Americans Changed

1) **Black actors** and **musicians** had **more recognition** in this period, as African Americans began to **assert themselves**.
2) **African Americans** on **television** and in films were **less likely** to be portrayed as **slow-witted** and **subservient**, instead they were given **leading roles** and their characters were often **professional** and **intelligent**. For example, **Sidney Poitier** played a **detective** in the film ***In the Heat of the Night*** (**1967**) and **Bill Cosby** starred as an undercover **CIA agent** in the TV series ***I Spy*** between **1965** and **1968**. Cosby was given his **own show** in **1969** — ***The Bill Cosby Show***.
3) In **1968** the **musician James Brown** released the single ***Say it Loud — I'm Black and I'm Proud***, after the **assassination** of **Martin Luther King**. Brown's song became an anthem for **African American empowerment**.

Practice Questions

Q1 Give some examples of the cultural impact of Black Power.

Exam Question

Q1 Why was the Black Power movement so popular in the late 1960s? [30 Marks]

Black Power at the Olympics...

At the 1968 Mexico Olympics, two African American athletes, Tommie Smith and John Carlos, performed Black Power salutes (holding a clenched fist in the air above them) on the podium. Their actions got them thrown out of the Olympics.

The Black Panthers

The Black Panthers were a part of the Black Power movement. They called for the use of violence to transform the US. Their ideology was a mixture of socialism and black nationalism that appealed to many African Americans.

The **Black Panthers** were a **Radical Organisation**

1) The **Black Panther Party for Self-Defense** was **founded** in **1966** by **Huey Newton** and **Bobby Seale**. It **originated** in **California**, but rapidly **spread across America**.
2) The Panthers were **never** a **large organisation** — they never reached **10 000 members** — but their **statements** and **actions** won them **respect** and **notoriety**.
3) The **Panthers' uniform** of **black beret**, **black leather jacket** and **sunglasses** made them an **instantly recognisable presence** in the ghettos.
4) The Panthers believed in self-defence and the **right to carry guns** — **Chinese communist** leader Mao Zedong's famous phrase, "**power grows out of the barrel of a gun**", became a popular slogan. In **1967**, **30 armed Panthers marched** in **Sacramento**, **California**, to **protest** a **bill** which **proposed restricting** people from **carrying guns** in **public**.

A Black Panther march in 1968.

5) The Panthers used **strong**, **abusive language** — it gave them a '**tough**' **image** and made them seem **very different** from traditional civil rights organisations like the **NAACP**.

The **Panthers** had a **Ten-Point Programme**

1) The **Black Panthers' ideology** was **influenced** by **Malcolm X**, and who championed **violent self-defence**. The Panthers believed in **arming themselves** to **defend** their **communities** against **police violence**, and they **opposed** King's methods of **peaceful protest** and **cooperation** with **white politicians**.
2) The ideas of philosopher **Karl Marx**, who wrote about how the **revolution** of the **working classes** would lead to the **creation** of an **equal society**, were a **key part** of the **Panthers' revolutionary ideology**. The Panthers wanted to lead a **revolution** of the **working class** in America, and put an end to inequality.
3) The Panthers created a **Ten-Point Programme**, which covered a **wide range** of **issues** that they wanted solving. The first point, which was **influenced** by **Black Power**, called for African Americans to have the **power** and **freedom** to **determine** their **futures**. Moreover, the Panthers wanted **black history** and **black culture** to be **taught** in **schools**.
4) **Several points** referred to **improving** the **economic** and **social inequalities** that **African Americans faced**. For example, the Panthers called for **free health care**, **full employment**, **decent housing** and **education** (which taught the **history** of **African Americans**), as well as **financial compensation** for **centuries** of **slavery** and **oppression**.
5) The Panthers also wanted an **end** to **police brutality**, and for **African Americans** in **prison** to be **released**. They argued that African Americans accused of **crimes** should be **tried** in front of a **jury** of **fellow African Americans**.

The **Panthers** organised a lot of **Programmes**

1) The **Panthers operated** a '**Patrol the Pigs**' programme, where Panthers **patrolled ghettos** in order to **deter police harassment**, especially of **young African Americans**. **Huey Newton** and other Panthers often **questioned** the **police** to see if they were **abusing** their **power**, but these confrontations sometimes led to **violent clashes**.
2) The **Panthers** created '**survival programmes**', which were **very popular**, such as the **Free Breakfast programme** which provided **meals** for **thousands** of children in the **ghettos**. The Panthers believed that a **breakfast** would help children **study better** at **school**.
3) **Free health clinics** set up by the Panthers carried out **testing** for **sickle cell anaemia** — a condition which affects many **African Americans**. The Panthers also ran **drug** and **alcohol awareness programmes**.
4) The Panthers set up '**liberation schools**', which were run by **volunteers**. They taught **black history** and the **achievements** of **black people**. The schools aimed to **promote racial pride** and **self-confidence**.
5) The Panthers also organised **voter registration drives** to get **African Americans** in the **ghettos** to **vote**.

The Black Panthers

Despite the small size of the organisation, the Black Panthers had a big reputation and attracted the attention of the government. The party was attacked by the FBI in an attempt to destroy it, and it had its own internal problems too.

The Panthers received a lot of Criticism

1) The **head** of the **FBI**, **J. Edgar Hoover**, stated in **1969** that the **Panthers** were the **"greatest threat to the internal security of the country"**. He was **determined** to **destroy them**.
2) **Roy Wilkins**, **head** of the **NAACP**, was **opposed** to the **violence** advocated by the **Panthers**. He believed that it was **African Americans** who ultimately **suffered** from **black militancy** because it damaged their communities.
3) The Panthers were often accused of **sexism** — the **prominence** of **Eldridge Cleaver**, a **convicted rapist**, and the Panthers' **macho** image **alienated** many **black women**.

The Panthers were Targeted by the Government

1) The **FBI's counter-intelligence unit**, **COINTELPRO**, believed that the **Panthers** were a **dangerous revolutionary group**, so they began to **illegally disrupt** their **activities**.
2) The **FBI** tried to find **evidence** to **destroy** the **Panthers**. They **tapped** the **phones** and **bugged** the **offices** and **homes** of **Black Panther Party leaders**. The **FBI** also **paid informants**, used agents to **infiltrate** the **organisation**, and tried to **incite violence** between **members** of the **Panthers**, and between the **Panthers** and **other gangs**.
3) The Panthers also **split internally**. In **1968**, **Huey Newton** and **Eldridge Cleaver**, a **senior member** of the **Black Panther Party**, argued over the **Panthers' tactics**. **Newton** wanted the Panthers to **focus** on the **survival programmes**, whereas **Cleaver** wanted the Panthers to use **more violence**.
4) By **1970**, after **several gunfights** with the **police**, **internal conflict** and the **unconstitutional harassment** conducted by the **FBI**, many of the **main** Panther **leaders** had been **arrested** or **killed**. The Black Panthers **faded away** in the **1970s** and **dissolved** in **1982**.

The Panthers had Some Success

The Panthers were a **small organisation**, but they had a **significant impact** in this period.

1) The **notoriety** of the **Panthers** meant that people **took notice** of them, and their **ideology** of **black nationalism** strongly **appealed** to many **African Americans**. For example, **support** for the Panthers among **black soldiers** in **Vietnam** was **widespread**.
2) The Panthers helped many **young black people** to develop a sense of **identity**, and the Panthers were regarded by some as the **embodiment** of **Black Power**.
3) The Panthers ultimately **rejected black nationalism**, condemning it as **black racism**. They believed that they should **lead** a **revolution** of **all races**.
4) The **survival programmes** were **successful** — the **free breakfast** and **free clinics programmes** helped thousands of people.
5) They also had a **major influence** on **radical elements** of the **Hispanic** and **Native American** civil rights movements (see pages 36-37).

The 'Black Kittens' didn't inspire young radicals.

Despite the **good work** performed by the **Panthers**, **some** of its **leading members** were **convicted** of **murder** and other **criminal activity**. The Panthers **murdered** one of their **own members** whom they **suspected** of being an **FBI informant**.

Practice Questions

Q1 Briefly describe the ideology of the Black Panther Party.

Q2 Give two examples of 'survival programmes' set up by the Black Panthers.

Q3 Why were the Panthers targeted by the government?

The Black Panthers — a roaring success...

... well, sort of. The Black Panthers never gained mass membership, but they were influential in the ghettos and they won respect for their survival programmes. They were undone by a mix of FBI trickery and their own violent internal squabbling.

Introduction to Section 4

The last introduction page — don't waste it. Get those key dates, important people and historical vocab firmly lodged into your brain. Don't push them in too hard though — we don't want any accidents.

Here's a **Quick Summary** of **Section Four**

This section deals with the **American protest culture** and **Hispanic American**, **Native American** and **women's rights**. Here's some information to get you started:

- A **protest culture** developed in American during the **1960s**, mainly among **young people**. Many Americans **protested against** the **Vietnam War**, and **racial** and **sexual discrimination**.
- **Hispanic Americans** campaigned for **greater civil rights** in the 1960s. They used many of the **same tactics** as the **African Americans** to press for change. **Cesar Chavez** attempted to **improve farm workers' rights**.
- **Native Americans** also fought against **discrimination**. They **copied** the **tactics** of **African Americans** too, but their aim **wasn't** to **integrate** with other races — they wanted to **keep** their **cultural identity**.
- **American women** were also **unhappy** with being **discriminated against**. **Feminists** like **Betty Friedan** and **Eleanor Roosevelt** promoted **women's rights** and **women's liberation**.

Learn the **Key Dates** of the **Ethnic Minorities** and **Women's Rights Campaigns**

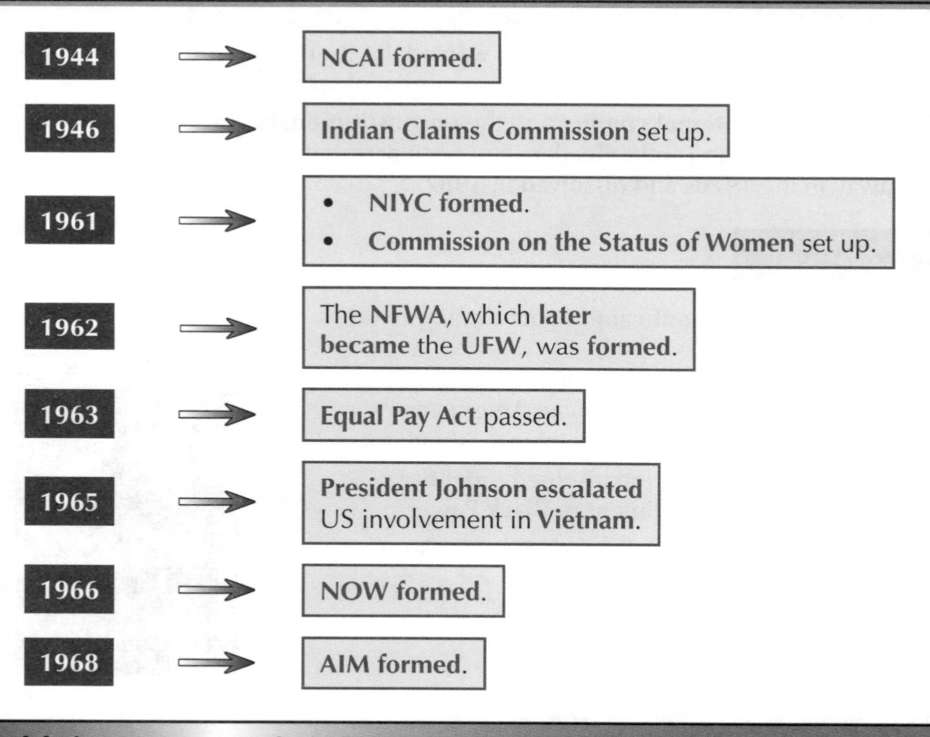

Important People in this Period:

- **Cesar Chavez** — Hispanic American civil rights activist.
- **Betty Friedan** — Feminist activist and author of *The Feminine Mystique*.
- **Eleanor Roosevelt** — Feminist activist and widow of President Roosevelt.
- **President Richard M. Nixon** — US President, 1969-1974.

Make sure you know what these **Historical Terms** mean

- **UFW** — United Farm Workers is an organisation that was set up by Cesar Chavez. It was the first farm workers' union in the US.
- **Brown Berets** — A Hispanic American organisation similar to the Black Panthers.
- **NCAI** — The National Congress of American Indians is similar to the NAACP. It challenged racial discrimination in the courts.
- **Termination** — The US government's policy of trying to get Native American tribes to give up their legal existence.
- **NIYC** — The National Indian Youth Council was created by young Native Americans. Its members took direct action against discrimination.
- **AIM** — The American Indian Movement is a militant organisation influenced by the Black Panthers.
- **NOW** — The National Organisation for Women was set up by Betty Friedan to campaign for women's liberation.

Protest Culture and Vietnam

Young Americans became very politicised in the 1960s, and often held demonstrations about the major issues of their time — be it civil rights, the Vietnam War or equality for women. Others, like hippies, refused to conform. Far out...

Important Changes took place in the US After 1945

1) From 1945 the US economy **grew rapidly** and many white Americans became very **affluent**.
2) **Highway building programmes** in the **1950s** led to the **growth** of **suburbs**, and by the **1960s most Americans owned** their **own homes**. Many Americans had **well-paid jobs** which enabled them to live **comfortable** lives surrounded by **new possessions**, such as **televisions**, **washing machines** and **cars**.
3) **President Kennedy** and his **successor**, President **Johnson**, both developed policies to **improve US society**. Kennedy's **New Frontier programme** sought **improvements** in **education** and **health care**, while **Johnson's Great Society programme** provided **billions** of **dollars** for **schools**, **housing** and **health care**.
4) After the Second World War there was a **baby boom** in the US, which meant that by the **1960s** there was a **large population** of **teenagers**. These young Americans were more **politically aware** than their parents' generation. This was because they'd received a **good education** and because of the **increasing availability** of **television**, which enabled them to **witness** the **prejudice** displayed **against African Americans**, and some of the horrors of the **Vietnam War**.

The Youth in America were Politically Active

The **privileged economic position** of many young Americans meant that they **didn't** have to get **jobs** straight after school, and could go to **university**. This gave them the ability to become **involved** in **campaigns**.

1) In **1960**, **students** in **Michigan** formed the **Students for a Democratic Society** (**SDS**), an **organisation** that campaigned for **economic equality**. The **SDS** were part of a **growing movement** in the **1960s** known as the '**New Left**' — a term used to describe **organisations** led by **young radicals** who wanted a more **equal society** in the **US**.
2) The **SDS** led high-profile campaigns **against** the **Vietnam War**.

- In **March 1965 President Johnson escalated** the **US's involvement** in **Vietnam**, sending **thousands** of **young American men** to **fight** the **communists**.
- In **April 1965** the SDS led an anti-war protest of around **20 000** people in **Washington, D.C.**
- The SDS were also involved with several other **anti-war protests** including **teach-ins** where teachers and students debated the war rather than having lessons.
- **Students** formed a strong opposition to the war — many **feared** being **conscripted** into the army to fight in Vietnam. Some civil rights groups such as **SNCC** and **CORE** opposed the war too.
- The **Vietnam War** led to the **deaths** of **millions** of people — the US used **hugely destructive bombing** against the **North Vietnamese**, and sprayed **toxic defoliants** on the **jungle**. This made many young Americans **question** their **government's morality** and whether the **US** really was a **force for good**.

3) **Young Americans**, particularly those who went to college, also got involved with the **civil rights movement**, **women's liberation** organisations (see p.39) and **environmental** organisations such as **Friends of the Earth** (formed in **1969**).

A Counterculture Developed in America

1) Some young Americans **rejected** the **conformity** of **American society**, which **expected** people to **act** in a **certain way** (e.g. get jobs, get married, raise children). These people formed the **counterculture movement**.
2) The **counterculture movement** included groups like **hippies** (young people who didn't want to conform to what mainstream society expected), **anti-war campaigners** (such as the SDS) and **feminists** (campaigners for women's rights). They had different beliefs and aims, but they all **challenged** the **social** and **cultural norms** of **1960s America**.
3) **Music** was an important part of the counterculture. **Criticism** of the **Vietnam War** and of **US society** was common in **1960s music**. **Bob Dylan's** song ***The Times They Are A-Changin'*** summed up the feeling that there was a **youth-led rebellion** which would **create** a **different society**.
4) A **drugs** culture developed in the **1960s**. The **psychedelic music** of artists like **Jimi Hendrix** was influenced by the **hallucinogenic** drug **LSD**.

Hippies — living the high life dude...

The hippies symbolised the new cult of individualism in the 1960s. Hippies refused to conform with the norms of society — some experimented with drugs, wore long flowing clothes and flowers. They also promoted the slogan 'make love, not war'.

Hispanic Americans

You need to remember that it wasn't just African Americans who were campaigning for civil rights in this period. Hispanic Americans were also treated like second-class citizens, and they formed organisations to campaign for change.

*Many **Mexicans Settled** in **America** in the **Early 20th Century***

1) During the **early 20th century**, many **farmers** in the **south** and **west** of the **US** relied on **large-scale immigration** from **Mexico**, which provided men and women to work as **agricultural labourers.** By **1930** around **1.5 million ethnic Mexicans** were living in the US.
2) **Labour shortages** in **World War Two increased** the **flow** of **unskilled immigrants**. Mexican labourers worked **long hours** in the fields and were **paid less** than their **American counterparts**. However, **wages** in **America** were **better** than they were in **Mexico** and **immigration grew rapidly** between **1945** and **1968**.
3) **Mexican Americans** found it hard to integrate into **US society** because they spoke **Spanish** and had a **different cultural identity** to **most Americans**.

Cultural identity is the beliefs, traditions, history and language that belong to a certain group.

*Hispanic Americans **Demanded Better Treatment***

1) From the **early 1950s**, **Hispanic Americans** began to organise themselves to demand **better working** and **living conditions**, and to secure **basic civil rights**. In **1951** the **American Council of Spanish-speaking People** (**ACSSP**) was formed to **combat discrimination** in areas such as **housing**, **employment** and **education**.
2) **After** the **Brown v Board of Education** ruling (see pages 12-13), the **ACSSP** and the **NAACP** occasionally worked together to **desegregate schools**.
3) **Cesar Chavez** campaigned for the **rights** of **farm workers**, many of whom were **Hispanic**. The farm workers were **very poorly paid** and had **few labour rights**. From **1952** he began to organise **voter registration drives** and campaigned against **racial discrimination** towards **Hispanic Americans**.
4) In **1962 Chavez** formed the **National Farm Workers Association** (**NFWA**), which later became **United Farm Workers** (**UFW**) — the first farm union in the US. The **NFWA** used non-violent direct action, such as **boycotts**, **peaceful protests** and **pickets** (peaceful crowds that act as a barrier), to campaign for **improved rights** for **farm workers**. In **1965** it began a **prolonged strike**, which secured **higher wages** for **workers** on large **commercial grape farms**.
5) The **Mexican American Political Association** (**MAPA**) was formed in **1960**. It aimed to provide **political empowerment** for **Chicanos** (**Mexican Americans**) through **voter registration drives** and campaigns to **elect Mexican American politicians**.

Hispanic American Organisations became more Radical in the late 1960s

1) Some Hispanic Americans formed **radical organisations** like the **Young Chicanos for Community Action** (**YCCA**). The **YCCA** evolved into the **Brown Berets**, who had **similar tactics** to the **Black Panthers** (see pages 32-33).
2) The Brown Berets wore **army-style uniforms** and **monitored** the **police** to make sure they didn't harass Hispanic Americans. They also worked on **community programmes** to **improve housing**, **education**, **employment** and **health care**, and **protested against** the **Vietnam War**.
3) In **March 1968** the **Brown Berets** organised a series of '**school dropouts**', known as the '**Chicano Blowouts**', in which Hispanic American students **left** their **classes** to **protest against** the **poor standard** of their **education**.
4) The Brown Berets suffered from a **lack** of **clear aims**, **police harassment** and **in-fighting**. They **dissolved** in **1972**.
5) In the **late 1960s**, young Hispanic Americans from **Puerto Rico** formed the **Young Lords**. The **Young Lords** were **similar** to the **Black Panthers** — they organised **community campaigns** and tried to stop **police harassment** of Hispanic Americans. They also campaigned for **women's equality**.

- In the years **1945** to **1968 Hispanic Americans** started to **challenge racial discrimination** against them. Organisations like **MAPA** and individuals like **Cesar Chavez** made **some improvements** to the lives of Hispanic Americans. Furthermore, the work of **African American civil rights organisations** in **overturning segregation** and securing the **1964** and **1965 Civil Rights Acts** gave Hispanic Americans greater **legal rights**.
- However, the **rise** of **radicalism** among **Hispanic Americans** shows that many were still **frustrated** by the **economic** and **social status** of **Hispanic Americans**. Despite **voter registration drives**, Hispanic Americans were **under-represented** among American voters, which meant they had **little political power**.

Native Americans

Like the Hispanic Americans, the Native Americans were inspired by the African American civil rights movement.

Life Changed for Native Americans after the Second World War

1) In **1945**, most of the **Native American population** of the US (around **350 000** people), lived on **reservations — land set aside** for **different Native American tribes**. On the reservations Native Americans had their **own governments** with powers in areas such as **law** and **order**.
2) The **Bureau of Indian Affairs** oversaw the **tribes**, and provided them with things such as **health care**. However, in **1943** a **government survey** of the **reservations reported** that **most Native Americans lived** in **extreme poverty**.
3) During the **Second World War**, thousands of Native Americans **left** their **reservations** to fight or to work in factories, and **experienced American life** and **culture** for the first time. After the war, many **Native Americans** continued to leave and **moved** to the **cities**, but they **struggled** to get **well-paid jobs** or a **good education** for their children.
4) The **National Congress of American Indians** (**NCAI**) was formed in **1944** to **fight** for Native American **rights**. The **NCAI followed** the **NAACP's tactic** of **challenging discrimination** in the **courts**.
5) The **Indian Claims Commission** was **established** by the government in **1946**. It provided Native Americans with some **compensation** for the **lands** they'd **lost** to the **government**. The Commission **awarded $800 million** in **compensation** between **1946** and **1978**.

President Eisenhower introduced the policy of 'Termination' in the 1950s

1) **Termination** was introduced to tackle **poverty** among Native Americans. The **government pushed individual tribes** to **agree** to **give up** their **legal existence** so that **Native Americans** would be like **any other US citizens**.
2) The government offered to **buy reservations** and **redistribute** the **money** to the Native Americans. The government also **helped Native Americans integrate** into **US society** — a **relocation programme** was **offered** which included **financial incentives** to **encourage** them to **move** to **towns** and **cities**.
3) However, like African Americans, the **Native Americans** experienced **discrimination** and **hardship** in the **cities**. Many Native Americans **struggled** to **adjust** to **urban life**, and **suffered** due to **unemployment** and **alcoholism**.
4) Many Native Americans felt that **termination threatened** their **cultural identity**, and so the **NCAI** campaigned **against** it. In 1970 **President Richard Nixon ended** the **termination policy**.

Native American Activists became more Militant in the 1960s

1) In **1961** the **National Indian Youth Council** (**NIYC**) was established. NIYC was **more radical** than the **NCAI** and, following the example of the civil rights movement, decided that **direct action** was **more** likely to be **successful** than the **NCAI's legal tactics**. For example, NIYC organised **'fish-ins'** as a way of **asserting** their **right** to **fish** in several rivers.
2) In **1968** the **American Indian Movement** (**AIM**) was founded. It adopted the same **aggressive approach** used by the **Black Panthers** (see pages 32-33), and used the slogan **'Red Power'**. Inspired by the **Panthers**, **AIM patrolled neighbourhoods** wearing **red jackets** and **berets**, and **monitored police harassment** of **Native Americans**.
3) In **1969** a group called the **Indians of All Tribes** (**IAT**) occupied the disused prison on **Alcatraz Island** in **California**. They claimed the **island belonged** to **Native Americans**, not the US government. The remaining protesters were **removed** in **1971** by **US government officers**.

Between **1945** and **1968**, **Native Americans** made **some progress** in **challenging racial discrimination**, but many **Native Americans** still faced a great deal of **poverty**. However, despite the policy of **termination**, **Native Americans** still maintained their **separate languages** and **cultural identities**.

Practice Question

Exam Question

Q1 To what extent did the African American civil rights movement benefit Hispanic and Native Americans? [30 Marks]

Berets — apparently you can't be a radical unless you've got one...

Groups such as the Brown Berets and AIM gave a sense of racial pride to many Hispanic and Native Americans. However, there were divisions within the Hispanic and Native American movements, in part because they were from different countries or tribes.

Women's Liberation

Like the Hispanic and Native Americans, American women were inspired by the African American civil rights movement to fight for their own rights. Women had to struggle against the media's portrayal of their role in society.

Women Supported the War Effort

1) **During** the **Second World War, millions of women worked** in **factories** for the **first time** in their lives. In addition, **350 000 women served** in the **armed forces.**
2) **US propaganda highlighted** the **importance** of **women's** contribution to the **war effort.**
3) **After 1945**, many **women lost** their **jobs** as **millions** of **ex-servicemen** returned to the **workplace.**
4) **Most women** who wanted to continue working had **limited job opportunities**, and could often only find low-paid work as **shop assistants** or **secretaries.**
5) However, by **1956 35%** of **adult women** were in **paid employment.**

The Media in the 1950s showed Women as Mothers and Housewives

1) In the **postwar years**, **especially** during the **affluent 1950s**, the **media portrayed women** as **dutiful housewives**, **mothers** and **homemakers**.
2) **Television shows** such as ***I Love Lucy*** **emphasised** a **woman's role** as a **housewife**, and **women's magazines** focused on **motherhood** and **homemaking** — they implied that women should let their **husbands** make the **important decisions** for the family, and that women should **support** their decisions.
3) **Marriage** was shown as being the **most important** thing for a **woman** to achieve. It **wasn't** unusual for a girl to **marry before** she was **20** and to go on to have a **large family**.
4) One **result** of **early marriage** was that many **young women** didn't **graduate** from **university**. In **1960**, only **37%** of **women** who attended university actually **graduated** — many who **dropped out** did so in order to **marry**.
5) **However**, by the **end** of the **1950s** many women were **unhappy** with their **low status** in **society**, and with the **dull everyday routine** of being housewives and mothers. **Doctors reported** that many **housewives slept** for up to **ten hours** a **day**, and **millions** were **taking tranquillizers** to relieve their **unhappiness** and **boredom**.

Women were Discriminated Against in the Workplace

1) Those women who **worked for a living** were **paid less** than their **male colleagues**. **Women** were usually **confined** to **certain professions**, such as **secretarial work**, **nursing**, **waitressing** and **teaching**.
2) In **1961 President Kennedy** established a **Commission on the Status of Women**, chaired by **President Roosevelt's widow**, **Eleanor**. The **Commission reported** that there was **widespread discrimination** against women:

- **Women didn't** receive **equal pay** to men for **equal work**.
- **Employers** often **refused** to **hire women**.
- In **1960** only **7%** of **doctors** and **around 4%** of **lawyers** were **women**.

Eleanor Roosevelt

3) Things did **improve** for **women** — in **1963 Kennedy passed** the **Equal Pay Act**, which **guaranteed equal pay** for **men** and **women** who **performed** the **same duties**, while the **1964 Civil Rights Act outlawed discrimination** against women in the field of **employment**.
4) However, these **laws** were **often ignored** in practice, so women began to set up their own **women's liberation groups** to **campaign** for real **change**.

Women's Liberation

Life could be very unfulfilling for housewives stuck in suburbia, while those women who did work were discriminated against. Feminists like Betty Friedan took up the struggle for equality for women.

Betty Friedan led the Campaign for Equality

1) In **1963 Betty Friedan** published the **influential book**, ***The Feminine Mystique***. In it she claimed that **women** were **suffering** because they were told by the **media** that they should feel **fulfilled** as **housewives** and **mothers** — women who **didn't** feel fulfilled by this life felt like **failures**.
2) Friedan accused **television**, **women's magazines** and **advertisers** of creating a **false image** of **women**, and called on women to press for **change**. As **more women** got **jobs** they felt **increasingly empowered** to **demand equality**.
3) In **1966 Friedan** set up the **National Organisation for Women** (**NOW**), which was termed **"an NAACP for women"**. **NOW used** many of the **NAACP's techniques**, including **lawsuits** and **boycotts**.
4) **NOW** campaigned against **discrimination** in **employment** and managed to press **President Johnson** to sign **Executive Order 11375 in 1967**. This made **sexual discrimination illegal** for companies doing work for the government.
5) NOW also successfully appealed to the **Equal Employment Opportunity Commission** (**EEOC**), which was formed in **1965**, to stop **airline companies** from **sacking female cabin crew members** when they **married** or **turned 32**.

Women became Very Politically Active in the 1960s

1) More and more women began to **identify themselves** as **feminists** — people who **campaigned** for **equal rights** for women — and they **engaged** in the **political issues** of the era. Women were **influential** in **demonstrations against** the **Vietnam War** and **in favour** of **African-American civil rights**.
2) However, women were often treated unequally in organisations such as **SNCC** and the **SDS** (see p.35), which were often **sexist** and **patronising**. Female activists **complained** that while **American men** showed **empathy** for the **Vietnamese** or **African Americans**, they **showed none** for American **women**.
3) When **SNCC expelled** its **white members** in **1966**, many of its former white female members **joined** either **NOW** or the more **radical feminist organisations**. These women brought with them the **tactics** they'd developed in **direct action** and **community campaigning**.

Women's Groups became more Radical in the Late 1960s

1) Radical feminists **rejected** what they saw as a **male-dominated society** and the **institutions** of that society, such as **marriage** and **family**. They felt that women should **lead** their **own society**.
2) In **1967**, feminists in **New York** formed the **New York Radical Women** (**NYRW**). In **1968** NYRW organised a **demonstration against** the **Miss America pageant** in **Atlantic City**, **New Jersey**. **NYRW members** crowned a **sheep** as their own **'Miss America'**.
3) Feminists made some **progress** by the end of the **1960s**:
   - **Men** and **women** were treated more equally at **work**.
   - **NOW campaigned** for the **legalisation** of **abortion** in the **US**, and in **1973** the **Supreme Court ruled against** state **bans** on **abortion** (Roe v Wade).
4) However, **ingrained attitudes** towards women, especially views on the **role** of **women** in the **home**, were **slow** to **change**. Many women were **uneasy** about **feminism** and some **opposed** it.

Practice Questions

Q1 How did Betty Friedan contribute to the women's liberation movement?

Exam Question

Q1 How successful was the women's liberation movement in achieving its aims in the 1960s? [30 Marks]

And start revising — NOW...

You might be asked a question on how the African American civil rights movement impacted on women's fight for equality, so remember — the 1964 Civil Rights Act gave equal rights to women. Head over to Section 5 — I've got a treat for you (not really...).

The Exam

Your exam is 'Unit 1 — Historical Themes In Breadth — Option D — A World Divided: Communism and Democracy in the 20th Century'. A bit of a mouthful. Polar bears don't do exams, but if they did, they'd be brrrrilliant...

You have to answer **Two Questions** in **1 Hour** and **20 Minutes**

1) The exam paper has questions on **seven topics**. You will have **studied two** of them, so you can **ignore** the rest.
2) You need to know the **name** and **number** of the **topics** you have studied, e.g. D5 — Pursuing Life and Liberty: Equality in the USA, 1945-68.
3) **Each** topic has a choice of **two questions** — you only need to answer **one** of them.
4) The exam is **1 hour 20 minutes** — that gives you **40 minutes per question**.
5) **Each question** is worth **30 marks** — so they're **equally important**.

Great hair gave Tim the confidence to ace his exam.

Don't Rush — **Read** the question and **Plan** your answer

At the start of the Exam

- Look at **both** questions **carefully** and decide which you will find **easier** to answer. Read the **whole question** and not just the key words — the question might be different to what you were expecting.
- Spend about **5 minutes thinking** about what the question is asking you for and jot down **important points**.

During the Exam

- **Answer the question.** Don't write an answer to a question you've memorised — **answer the question in the exam paper**. Keep **referring back** to the question in your answer — that way you won't get sidetracked.
- Keep an **eye on the time**. You'll **lose marks** if you spend an hour on the first question and only leave yourself 20 minutes for the second one.

At the end of the Exam

- If you have time at the end, **check through** your **answers**. Make any corrections **neat** and **obvious** — it makes it easier for the examiner to see your changes.

The Exam **Also** tests **How** you **Write**

You're writing for **someone else**, so don't make it hard for the examiner to understand what you're saying.

1) Structure your essay in **paragraphs** (see p.43).
2) Write in an **appropriate style**. This is a **formal** exam, so it's **not** a good idea to use slang, chatty language or text speak.
3) The examiner will consider your **spelling** and **grammar** when deciding your mark, so make sure your essay is easy to **read** and **understand**.
4) Use **historical terms** which link to your module — e.g. **civil rights**, **segregation**, **Black Power**.
5) Write **neatly** — the examiner **can't give** you **marks** if they **can't read** what you've **written**.

You best be usin' proper grammar now — proper grammar is proper good...

If you didn't already know, the examiner is not your friend — they're evil aliens from a far-away planet sent to make students' lives miserable... Anyway, the point is they're not your friend, so don't talk to them like one, otherwise they'll mark you down. Harshly.

Mark Scheme

Mark Scheme — something that helps the examiner to figure out what level your exam answer is at so they can work out what mark to give it — and not the chief examiner's name. Easy mistake to make though...

Your answer will be given a **Level** from **1** to **5**

1) Each level has a description of the **key features** the examiner is **looking for** in your answer.
2) The examiner will try to **judge** which **level** your answer **matches best**.
3) The examiner will then decide what **mark** to give you **within** that **level**. For example, if the examiner thinks that you've written a **high level 3** answer, then you might be awarded **18 marks**.
4) Your **overall grade** will be **worked out later** after everyone's results have been collected.

This mark scheme is **similar** to the one the examiner uses:

Level	Description	Marks
1	Brief statements about the topic. Doesn't show a clear understanding of the question. Facts are wrong. A few sentences and paragraphs. Poorly written.	1-6
2	Brief statements showing some understanding of the question being asked. Some facts are correct. Written in paragraphs, but poorly written.	7-12
3	Shows understanding of the question. Facts will mostly be correct. Events may be described rather than explained, or explained in little detail. May not discuss points related to the question or only discuss one point without considering others. Written clearly and in paragraphs.	13-18
4	Understands the question and provides an explanation using well-structured paragraphs. Most facts will be accurate and used to support the explanation. Begins to reach conclusions. May not cover all the key points or the whole time period. Very well written.	19-24
5	Answers the question directly. Acknowledges a range of factors and shows an understanding of how factors and their relationships change over time. Considers virtually the whole time period. Points are developed and clearly explained. Facts are accurate and support the argument. Reaches a sensible conclusion. Written and structured excellently.	25-30

Beat all the levels, rescue the princess, complete the exam.

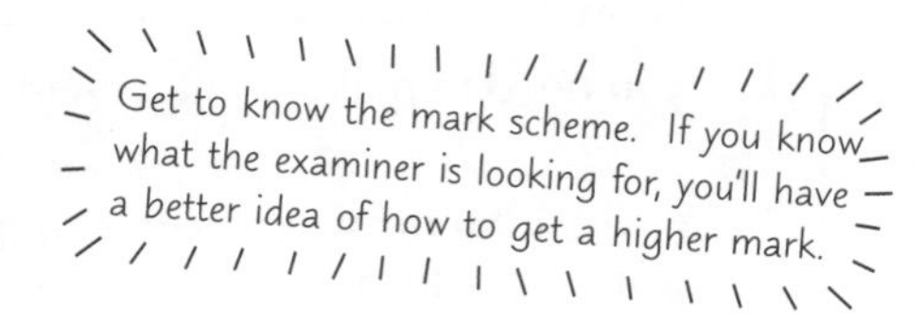

My best friends — Mark Scheme, Natalie Curriculum and Keeley Stage V

Basically, to get a good mark you need to answer the question. That sounds pretty obvious, but lots of people end up writing about what they know, and not what the question asks for. Answer the question properly and you should go far...

How to Structure Your Answer

Structuring your answer will keep you focused on the question. Knowing exactly what you are going to write will also make your answer flow much better. Exciting stuff this, and it could save your life... probably...

A **Good Introduction** shows that you **Understand** the **Question**

Your introduction sets the tone of your essay. Give the examiner a **good first impression**.

1) Identify what the **key factor** is going to be in your essay.
2) **Mention** other **factors, alternative arguments** or other **reasons**.
3) Show that you **know** the **significance** of the **time** and **people/events** in the question.

Don't spend **too long** on your introduction. Leave yourself **enough time** for the rest of the answer.

The **Main Paragraphs** develop your **Argument**

Your paragraphs need to be **clear** and **concise** so that the examiner can easily follow your argument.

1) Try to write **5-8** paragraphs in the main body of the essay.
2) Each paragraph should make a **new point** that **adds** to your argument.
3) **Support** your points with **evidence** and show how they link back to the **question**.
4) **Balance** your answer by showing how **other factors** were **more** or **less important** — or by making points which **argue against** the statement made in the question.

The **Conclusion** should **Answer** the question

A good conclusion shows the examiner that you've come up with your **own interpretation** of the question.

1) A conclusion is your **final answer** to the question, so it should **round off** all of your points.
2) **Sum up** the points you made in your main paragraphs. Show how **each point** was **relevant** to your answer.
3) You need to make a **judgement**, e.g.

   which **factor** was the **most important**, or which **short-term** and **long-term** factors had the **biggest impact** on an event.

Make sure you write a conclusion, even if you're running out of time. The examiner needs to see what judgement you've come to.

In conclusion — structure for success...

Plan your answer properly, focusing on the question being asked. Work out what your argument is going to be, and organise it so that there's one point per paragraph. And make sure your conclusion follows on nicely — it shouldn't introduce anything new, or go against everything you've just said — it should just be a nice summary of your argument and the points you've made.

How to Structure Paragraphs

Well-structured paragraphs are a recipe for success, but you could also try: a litre of cream, six eggs, ten tablespoons of sugar, a grating of nutmeg and a spoonful of treacle. Whisk it up and drink it down hot. Mmm... success...

*Paragraphs are the **Building Blocks** of your essay*

A paragraph should be **constructed** in the **same way** as an **essay**:

1) Make an **introductory** point.
2) **Support** your point with an **explanation** and **factual evidence**.
3) Make a **concluding** point.

Jeff had two excellent points.

Each Paragraph** needs to make a **Point

1) You **won't** get many marks if you just **retell** the events. Like this...

2) Instead, your opening sentence should address the question **directly**. Like this...

The **most important reason** for the outbreak of war was .... because ....

3) Try to **link** your paragraph to the previous one so your answer flows.

Useful words for linking points

- Firstly / Secondly...
- Another...
- Consequently...
- Further...
- Of lesser importance...

Support** your **Points** with **Evidence

1) You need to **find relevant factual evidence** and **examples** to **support** the points you make.
2) This will allow you to **develop** what you mean by giving a more **detailed explanation**.
3) It's best if you can find **two** or **three** factual **examples** to **support** each point that you make.

End** your paragraphs with a **Concluding Statement

1) **Sum up** the point you made in your paragraph and **weigh up** the **importance** of the factor you've been discussing.
2) **Link** the **last sentence** of the paragraph with what you're going to discuss in the **next paragraph**, e.g.

Political factors were important, but economic factors were more important.

Oh, what's the point of carrying on? Oooo — sample exam questions...

In a weird way, a paragraph is just like a mini essay. So your final answer will be an essay, full of mini essays... That's just confusing — forget I said anything. Let me start again. Write your paragraphs just like mini essays, and you should be fine. Much clearer.

Sample Multi-Factor Question

The most common type of question you'll encounter is the 'multi-factor' style question. This type of question will ask you to write about a number of different factors and how they have contributed to a historical event.

Multi-factor** questions ask you to think about **More** than **One Factor

1) This type of question will ask you to explain the **causes** (or sometimes the **consequences**) of a **historical event**.
2) You will need to **weigh up** the importance of the factor in the question in comparison with **other factors** you have learnt about.
3) In the conclusion you'll need to make a **judgement** as to how **important** the factor in the **question** actually is.

Multi-factor questions will contain phrases like:

- How far do you agree...
- To what extent...
- ... responsible for...
- ... the main cause...

***Highlight** the **Key Words** in the question*

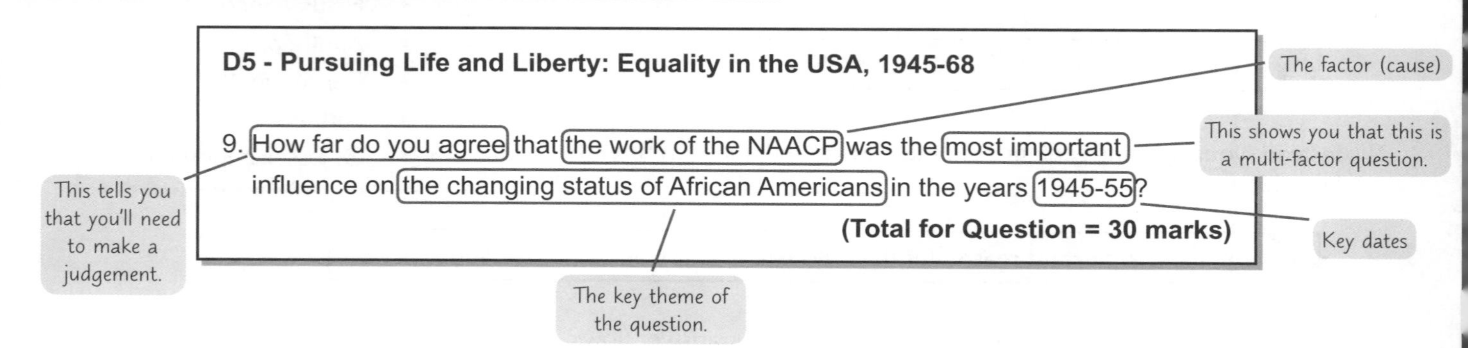

Pick out the **important bits** of the question so you can work **out** what it's asking you to do:

1) **The judgement** — e.g. 'How far do you agree'. The question is asking you to make a **judgement** about **how important** a certain factor was in **influencing changes** which occurred during a certain time period.
2) **The key theme** — e.g. 'the changing status of African Americans'. The **focus** will be on how certain **factors influenced** the **changes** in the **status** (e.g. position in society and politics) of **African Americans**.
3) **The factor in the question** — e.g. 'the work of the NAACP'. The question will identify the **main factor (influence)**, but it's **not** the **only** factor that you should **consider**.
4) **The time period** — e.g. '1945-55'. The question focuses on the **events** in the **years 1945** to **1955**, but **long-term factors (influences)** can **predate** these events by months or years.

*The **Examiner** wants you to...*

1) **Explain** the **importance** of the work of the **NAACP** in **influencing** the **changing status** of **African Americans** in the years **1945** to **1955**.
2) **Compare** the **importance** of this factor with **other** possible influences, e.g. you could mention the role of President Truman.
3) Make a **judgement** as to how far you agree that the work of the NAACP was the **most important factor**.
4) Show how it was **more** or **less important** than any **other** factors.

How to Select the Right Information

By the time you get to the exam you'll have learnt loads of facts, but you won't end up using most of them in your answers. Writing a good answer is all about selecting the right information from all the stuff in your head...

You need to look at **Why the NAACP** was **Important**

The question is **focused** on the **NAACP**, so you need information on them. However, the information must be **relevant** to the **question**, so **only** use things that are **related** to the **work** of the **NAACP** between **1945** and **1955**.

The points you'd use for this are on **Page 10**...

2) The NAACP aimed to **challenge segregation** in the **courts**. They hoped to secure **legal equality** for **African Americans** so that they **couldn't** be **treated differently** from **white US citizens**.
3) In **some cases** the NAACP used **other tactics**, such as **protests** and **boycotts**, to **highlight** certain **inequalities**.
4) NAACP membership **wasn't** restricted to African Americans — many of its members were **white** — but its campaigns focused on **African Americans**.
5) **Membership** of the **NAACP** grew **significantly** during the **Second World War**, and the organisation had about **450 000** members by **1945**. This allowed the **NAACP** to become **more active** in campaigning for civil rights.

You can use this to show that the NAACP was trying to improve the legal status of African Americans.

This shows that the NAACP had become very influential by 1945, and could conduct major civil rights campaigns.

1) The **NAACP** tried to get the US government to **honour** the **Fourteenth** and **Fifteenth Amendments** (see p.3) of the **US Constitution**. The Supreme Court had declared segregation legal in the **judgement** on **Plessy v Ferguson** (see p.4), so the **NAACP** aimed to **persuade** the **Supreme Court** to **reverse** its earlier decision and **force** Southern states to **repeal** their **Jim Crow** laws.
2) The **NAACP provided funding** and lawyers for **individuals** to bring cases **against** the **authorities**.
3) The **NAACP** also tried to **raise awareness** of their **cause** — they **appealed** to **politicians** in **Washington** for backing, **encouraged African Americans** to **register** to vote, and **organised** and **supported protests**.
4) Some African Americans felt that the NAACP's **methods** were **too slow** and they **didn't** change people's **attitudes**. The **NAACP wasn't** completely **opposed** to taking **direct action** to challenge racism, but felt that **widespread** and **lasting change** could **only happen** through the **Supreme Court**.

You could mention that the NAACP was trying to ensure that African Americans had the same legal status as white Americans, so they couldn't be treated as inferior.

This shows that some people felt that the NAACP's work wasn't improving the status of African Americans fast enough.

... and on **Page 11**...

Smith v Allwright — 1944

1) **Lonnie Smith** wanted to **vote** in the **Democrats' primary election** in **Texas**, but was **denied** the chance to vote because he was black.
2) A **primary election** is where a **political party's members choose** their **candidate** for an **election**. **Primary elections** were **important** in **Texas** because the **Democratic Party** was often the **only party** with a **chance** of winning, so the primary was the **only meaningful election** in the state.
3) **Thurgood Marshall** argued Smith's case and the **Supreme Court** ruled that white-only **primary elections violated** the **Fifteenth Amendment**.

This is an example you could use of the NAACP improving the status of African Americans. Although this case was in 1944, the ruling affected the status of African Americans between 1945 and 1955.

Morgan v Virginia — 1946

1) **Irene Morgan refused** to **give up her seat** to a **white passenger** while **travelling** on an **interstate bus** in **Virginia**. She was **fined**.
2) Marshall argued her case and the **Supreme Court** declared that **segregation** on **interstate buses** contradicted the **Fourteenth Amendment**.

It's worth mentioning the NAACP's focus on the Constitution — they tried to get the Supreme Court to recognise that African Americans had rights guaranteed by the Constitution.

Sweatt v Painter — 1950

1) **Heman Sweatt**, a black student, was **refused admission** to the **law school** at the **University of Texas**. The **NAACP** and Marshall took his case to the **Supreme Court**.
2) **Before** the case was heard a **separate law school** for African Americans was **hurriedly** built. However, the **Supreme Court** ruled that the new law school provided an **inferior education** and **poor facilities**, and that **Sweatt** should be **admitted** to the **University of Texas law school**.

This is another good example of the NAACP's work that you could use.

... and on **Page 12**

- In May 1954 the **Supreme Court** made a **unanimous** judgement — **segregated schools violated** the **Fourteenth Amendment**. The Court ruled that **all** children should have access to their **local school**, **regardless** of their **colour**. The Court **completely rejected** the **principle** of 'separate but equal' set down by **Plessy v Ferguson**.
- **Earl Warren**, Chief Justice of the Supreme Court, played a **key role** in **convincing** the other **Supreme Court judges** to **end segregation** in **education** and in securing a **unanimous verdict** from the judges.

It's important that you mention Brown v Board of Education and its significance, because it was the NAACP's most important achievement in this period.

You need to mention the role that other people and organisations played in the changing status of African Americans (for more see pages 46-47).

How to Select the Right Information

Look at how the NAACP was Less Important in this period

You should look at ways in which the **NAACP's work** didn't **improve** the **status** of **African Americans**. You could also look at the role played by **other civil rights organisations** and how they **contributed** to the **changing status** of **African Americans** between **1945** and **1955**.

You'll find this info on Page 12...

It's important to mention that despite the NAACP's success in getting legal change, this didn't necessarily lead to actual change for African Americans.

This shows that many white people in the South still didn't consider African Americans to be their equals.

1) After the **Supreme Court issued** its **decision**, **some** school districts **immediately obeyed** the **ruling**. However, **many states** simply **refused** to **accept** the **ruling**, and **progress** was **slow**.
2) **One reason** for the **slow progress** towards integrated schools was that the **Court** hadn't **set** any **timescale** for **obeying** its **ruling**, so **states** and **schools took their time**.
3) Many **white parents** wanted to **keep segregated schools** — they decided to **resist** the **Court's decision**.

... and on Page 13...

1) In **1955** the **NAACP** tried to get the **Supreme Court** to give a **clear timetable** for the **desegregation** of all schools.
2) The **Court** responded with what is known as the **Brown II ruling**. The Court was **unwilling** to **provide** a **timetable** — it was only prepared to declare that **desegregation** should be carried out "**with all deliberate speed**".
3) **Brown II** was a **disastrous decision** for the **NAACP**. By failing to set a **clear timetable** for the **integration** of **schools**, the **Court encouraged resistance** to its **verdict** in **Brown v Board of Education** across the **South**.

You can use the Brown II ruling as evidence that the NAACP wasn't always successful in its work.

This gives an example of a time when the NAACP's actions backfired, and Southern racists were able to avoid making improvements for African Americans.

... and on Page 11

You need to show in your essay that although the NAACP were able to improve the legal status of African Americans, it didn't necessarily lead to a de facto improvement in their status.

You should mention that CORE used more confrontational tactics than the NAACP. On the Journey of Reconciliation they tried to force the federal government to enforce the Supreme Court's ruling on Morgan v Virginia.

You can also show that CORE's confrontational approach wasn't more successful in helping African Americans than the work of the NAACP.

These judgements of the Supreme Court **provided legal** (**de jure**) **support** for **desegregation**, but it was **very difficult** to ensure that these decisions were **put into practice** to secure **real** (**de facto**) **change**.

1) The Congress of Racial Equality (**CORE**) was created in **1942**. It was a civil rights organisation set up to **oppose segregation** — especially in **restaurants** and **interstate transport**.
2) **Unlike** the **NAACP**, **CORE** strongly advocated **direct action**. In **1947**, **CORE** members undertook the **Journey of Reconciliation**. **Black** and **white** members **travelled together** on **interstate buses** in the **South** to show that the **Supreme Court's** ruling on **Morgan v Virginia wasn't** being **enforced**.
3) The **NAACP denounced** the **Journey of Reconciliation**, because it **feared** that **CORE's actions** would lead to **violence**, but it promised **legal assistance** to CORE members.
4) The **Journey of Reconciliation revealed** that Southern states were **ignoring** the **Supreme Court's ruling** against segregation on interstate buses. **Two black members** of **CORE** were sentenced to **thirty days** in **jail** and two of the **white members** were sentenced to **three months** in **jail** for refusing to sit in separate sections of the bus.
5) The **Journey of Reconciliation failed** to make any changes in the South, but it provided a lot of **publicity** for **CORE**, which **continued** its policies of **peaceful direct action** throughout the **1950s**.

How to Select the Right Information

You need to look at the **Role** of the **Federal Government** and **Other Factors**

You should look at whether the **federal government** played a **more important role** in the **changing status** of African Americans than the **NAACP** did, and consider whether **other factors contributed** as well.

You'll find this info on **Page 8**...

3) '**To Secure These Rights**' clearly stated that **racism** was **harmful** to the **country** and **not** in keeping with what **America** should **stand for** — **freedom** and **equality**.
4) **Over** a **million copies** of the **report** were **printed** by the **US government** and **private publishers**, and it was widely discussed in **newspapers** and on the **radio**.
5) In **January 1948** Truman gave his **State of the Union address** to **Congress**. In it he stated that he was going to secure the "**essential human rights** of our **citizens**". Truman also argued that **racial discrimination**, especially in **education**, in the **workplace** and at the **voting booths** was "**contrary** to **American ideals** of **democracy**".

You should mention the role of President Truman. He set up the Commission which wrote 'To Secure These Rights', which brought national attention to the problem of racism.

This shows that Truman was committed to helping African Americans.

... and on **Page 9**...

You could use these as examples of Truman's role in improving the status of African Americans.

- **Executive Order 9980** set up the **Fair Employment Board**. It enforced **equal opportunities** in **government organisations**, but it didn't have enough **funding** to **operate properly**.
- **Executive Order 10308** withheld **defence contracts** from firms which practised **discrimination**. It set up the **Committee on Government Contract Compliance** (CGCC) to **monitor** the awarding of **government contracts**.
- **Executive Order 9981** called for **racial equality** in the **armed forces**. Some officers were **reluctant** to carry out this order, but a **shortage** of **troops** during the **Korean War** meant that units **couldn't** be **segregated**.

You could look at the **Historical Context**

You'll find this info on **Page 8**...

The Cold War was also an important factor in helping the civil rights movement, because it made segregation an embarrassment that federal government needed to address.

3) After 1945 the **Cold War** developed, as the **US** and the **Soviet Union** competed **economically** and **politically** to **increase** their **influence** and **support** across the world. **Soviet propaganda** criticised the **poor treatment** of **African Americans** in the US.
4) **Truman** wanted the **Soviet Union** to allow **free** and **fair elections** in the countries of **Eastern Europe occupied** by the **Soviet Union's army**. However, he found it hard to **demand free elections** when this **freedom** was **denied** to **millions** of **African Americans**. Many Americans felt that **civil rights** had to be addressed in the US before they could **criticise** other countries' **lack** of **respect** for **human rights**.

... and on **Page 6**...

4) African Americans who worked in **factories** in the **North** received **higher pay** than they'd done as **farm labourers** in the **South**, but they had **little prospect** of working in more **highly skilled jobs**.
5) The **African Americans** who **migrated** to the cities began to develop their own **communities** and **cultural life**, which centred on their **churches** and other institutions such as **trade unions** and the **National Association for the Advancement of Colored People** (**NAACP**) (see p.4).
6) The **urbanisation** of African Americans helped them to **work together** to **campaign** for their **rights**, as they were gathered **closer together** into **larger communities**.

The mass migration of African Americans to the North caused a change in the economic status of many African Americans.

You could mention that urbanisation helped African Americans to organise campaigns to improve their rights.

... and on **Page 7**...

This shows that the concentration of African Americans in the North (where they could vote) gave them the ability to vote black politicians into power. These politicians could then work to improve the status of African Americans.

4) In the **North**, **black voters** comprised a **significant percentage** of the **electorate** in **some states**.
5) There were **so many** new **black voters** in the North that **shrewd politicians** tried to **appeal** to them. If **African Americans voted** in a **bloc** (voted **together**) for the **same candidate** then their votes could **determine** the **result** of an **election**.
6) The **impact** of **black voters** can be seen in the **election** of **black Congressman Adam Clayton Powell, Jr.**, in **1944**. **Black voters** were also **crucial** to **President Truman's re-election** in **1948**.

How to Plan Your Answer

This page will help you plan an answer to a multi-factor type question, like the one on page 44.

Use a **Plan** to **Structure** your **Argument**

Here's the question again:

> How far do you agree that the work of the NAACP was the most important influence on the changing status of African Americans in the years 1945-55?

You shouldn't spend more than **5 minutes** on your plan, so don't make it too detailed.
Here are some things it could include:

1) **2-3 points** about how the **work** of the **NAACP** was an **important influence** on the **changing status** of **African Americans.**
2) **1-2 points** about ways in which the **work** of the **NAACP** failed to **change** the **status** of **African Americans.**
3) **2-3 alternative factors** that might have **influenced** the **status** of **African Americans** in the years **1945-55**, with an assessment of whether they were **more** or **less important** than the **NAACP**.
4) Some notes on what your **conclusion** will be.

Then you can:

1) Identify any **links** between the points you've thought of.
2) **Decide** which factor you think was the **most important.**

Here's an **Example Plan**

Your plan probably won't be as big as this — we've written it out in full and included a few more points than you'll use in your essays.

Changing status of African Americans

1. Importance of the NAACP
- Challenged segregation in the courts. Important victories — Smith v Allwright (1944), Morgan v Virginia (1946), Sweatt v Painter (1950) and Brown v Board of Education (1954).
- Overturned principle of 'separate but equal'.
- Able to get African Americans to be legally considered as equal to white Americans on buses and in schools and won the right for African Americans to vote in primary elections.

2. NAACP less important
- De jure changes not followed by de facto changes, e.g. continued segregation.
- Failure of Brown II — unable to set timetable for desegregation.

3. Other factors
- Truman — 'To Secure These Rights' report. Executive Orders, e.g. desegregating the army.
- Supreme Court — sympathetic to civil rights, ruled against segregation.
- Work of CORE and Journey of Reconciliation.

4. Background factors
- Cold War — made Americans want to solve embarrassing issue of civil rights.
- Economic and social changes — migration to North meant African Americans had better paid jobs, lived in large urban communities.
- Voted in blocs — elected black politicians.

5. Conclusion
- The role of the NAACP was the most important factor because it secured improvements to the legal status of African Americans.
- The role of the federal government was also very important, especially the work of Truman, but it wasn't as important as the role of the NAACP.

Worked Answer

These pages will show you how to take an okay answer and turn it into a really good one. Simple as that.

*Use your **Introduction** to get off to a **Good Start***

These pages are all about how to word your sentences to impress the examiner, so we haven't included everything from the plan on page 48.

You might start with something like...

> In their campaign to improve the status of African Americans, the NAACP used the courts. The NAACP was successful in improving the legal status of African Americans on buses and in education. However, there were other influences on the changing status of African Americans in this period.

This intro is **okay** because it...
1) Mentions what the **NAACP** did to **improve** the **status** of **African Americans**.
2) Suggests that **other factors** were involved.

However, it **doesn't** show that you're addressing the **period of time** in the question. You could write:

> In the decade after the Second World War, the status of African Americans slowly began to change. The NAACP played an important role in creating that change by using the courts, particularly the Supreme Court, to improve the legal status of African Americans. The NAACP was able to get the Supreme Court to rule that segregation on interstate buses and in schools was unconstitutional, and to overturn the principle of 'separate but equal'.

Here you've given some examples of changes to the status of African Americans that the NAACP was able to achieve.

You could finish your intro by showing that you're going to talk about **other factors** as well:

You've identified other factors that could've influenced change for African Americans.

> However, there were other important factors in the civil rights struggle, such as the role of President Truman, the work of other groups (like CORE) and the importance of changing economic and social conditions.

*Make your **First Paragraph** about the **Key Factor***

You could begin with:

> The work of the NAACP was very influential in gaining some improvement in the status of African Americans. They successfully persuaded the Supreme Court to overturn segregation laws regarding interstate buses and education.

1) This paragraph **shows** the **main method** used by the NAACP to **improve** the **status** of **African Americans** and provides some examples of **success**. But it **doesn't** explain **how** these victories **changed** the **status** of **African Americans**.
2) To **improve** this you could explain **how** the NAACP's **legal campaigns** helped change the status of African Americans:

> The NAACP used the Supreme Court to challenge segregation and the principle of 'separate but equal'. The NAACP was successful in several cases, such as Morgan v Virginia (1946) which desegregated interstate bus travel, Sweatt v Painter (1950), which allowed an African American to attend a previously all-white law school due to the absence of equal facilities, and Brown v Board of Education (1954), which ruled that segregation in education was unconstitutional. These victories improved the legal status of African Americans by giving them the same rights as white Americans on interstate buses and in education.

Here you're showing that the NAACP's work was successful in improving the status of African Americans.

You could go on to write about the ways in which the **NAACP** was **less significant** in **improving** the **status** of **African Americans**. You could look at how the **de jure changes** that the NAACP brought about weren't immediately followed by **de facto changes**, as shown by the **Brown II** ruling and the **slow pace** of **desegregation**.

Worked Answer

You should write about **Other Factors**

You might start like this:

> There were also other important factors affecting the status of African Americans. President Truman set up the Commission which wrote the report 'To Secure These Rights'. Truman also used Executive Orders to strengthen the rights of African Americans.

1) This paragraph introduces another **factor** which was **influential** in affecting the status of black Americans — the **role** of **federal government**. It also includes some **examples** of what President Truman did.
2) You can make this **better** by explaining **how** federal government **changed** the **status** of African Americans.

> The federal government played a crucial role in the changing status of African Americans between 1945 and 1955. President Truman commissioned the report 'To Secure These Rights', which condemned racism and recommended equal voting and fair employment rights for African Americans. Truman also issued Executive Order 9981, which desegregated the American army without the approval of Congress, who would have voted against it. Executive Order 9981 gave African Americans equal status to white soldiers in the army.

Here you're giving evidence to support your point.

You could then write about the **role** that the **Supreme Court** played in the **changing status** of **African Americans**.

You could think about the **Context**

You could say:

It's a good idea to link your points back to the question like this.

> The Cold War influenced the US government's decision to improve the status of African Americans. The USSR's Cold War propaganda heavily criticised the US's democratic credentials because it did not treat its own citizens equally, which was very embarrassing for the US government.

This paragraph **introduces** a **new factor** but it doesn't explain why it was **important** in influencing a **change** in the **status** of **African Americans**. To **improve** this you could write:

> The US government made some efforts to improve the status of African Americans because of the Cold War rivalry between the US and the USSR. The USSR produced propaganda which criticised the US for its racism and claimed that the US couldn't be seen as the leader of the free world if its own people weren't free. President Truman wanted the USSR to allow free and fair elections in Soviet-occupied Eastern Europe, but it was difficult to make this demand when African Americans couldn't vote. Therefore, President Truman felt that action needed to be taken to improve the status of African Americans, so that it was no longer an embarrassment to the country.

Here you've shown how the historical context had an impact on the changing status of African Americans in this period.

1) This paragraph is **good** because it explains **why** this factor was **important**.
2) You could go on to write about **other factors** which **affected** the **status** of **African Americans**, such as the **social** and **economic changes** that African Americans experienced between **1945** and **1955**.

Worked Answer

Finish your essay in Style

Your conclusion should **summarise** the **key points** that you've made in each paragraph. If you've linked your paragraphs well then you'll have **created an argument**.

You could start with something like this:

> The NAACP was very significant in influencing the changing status of African Americans during the period 1945-55. By using legal tactics, the NAACP was able to establish that African Americans were constitutionally entitled to equal rights, and in the case of Brown v Board of Education they launched a successful attack on the 'separate but equal' principle set down by Plessy v Ferguson.

This shows that you're considering the question.

This is **good**, but you can then **create balance** by referring to **other factors**, by adding something like this:

> However, there were other important factors which contributed to the changing status of African Americans. The context of the Cold War encouraged the federal government to help African Americans and Truman issued several Executive Orders to improve their status. The Supreme Court, under Earl Warren, was supportive of civil rights in this period and gave the NAACP the opportunity to launch their successful challenge against segregated education in the Brown v Board of Education case. And the status of millions of African Americans also changed because they migrated to the North where economic, political and social conditions were better than in the South.

Here you're balancing your conclusion by looking at other factors.

This is **better** because it shows you've **considered** other factors in your conclusion.

You need to make a Judgement

You **won't** have **answered** the question until you've **explained** which factor you think was **most important**.

You could write your judgement like this:

Here you've made a firm judgement on which factor you think was the most important.

> The NAACP's work was the most important factor in influencing the change in the status of African Americans between 1945 and 1955.

1) This decision is **fine**. It shows that you think the **NAACP's work** was the **most important factor** influencing the changing status of African Americans in this period.
2) But, you can write a more **complex** conclusion like this:

> The work of the NAACP was definitely the most important factor in the changing status of African Americans between 1945 and 1955. Even if de facto changes were slow to take place, the de jure changes the NAACP secured lifted African Americans above the status of second-class citizens.

Here you've provided a clear explanation to the examiner as to why you think the NAACP was the most important influence on the changing status of African Americans.

This judgement shows a **higher level** of **analysis**. You've shown the examiner that you think the **NAACP** was the **most important factor** in **improving** the **status** of **African Americans**, and **justified** your **decision**.

Sample Single-Factor Question

Another type of question you might come across in the exam is the single-factor question. As you might have guessed, these questions will ask you to write about one factor or one historical event.

Make sure you Stick to the Point

1) This type of question is asking whether you **agree** or **disagree** with a statement, or whether something has **changed** or **developed** over time.
2) You might also have to make a **judgement** about an individual, action, policy or idea.

Single-factor questions will begin with phrases like:

- How successful was...
- Do you agree that...
- How significant was...
- To what extent...

1) A single factor question may ask you about the **importance** of a **single** event, organisation or individual. So you can either:
    - Write about the ways in which the **single factor** was **significant** or **not significant**, or...
    - Write about how the **single factor** was **significant** and try to think of **other** more **significant factors**.
2) Or it will ask you whether a **single factor** has **changed over time**. So you should:
    - Write about the ways in which the **single factor changed**, and...
    - Write about the ways in which the **single factor stayed the same**.

Highlight the Key Words in the question

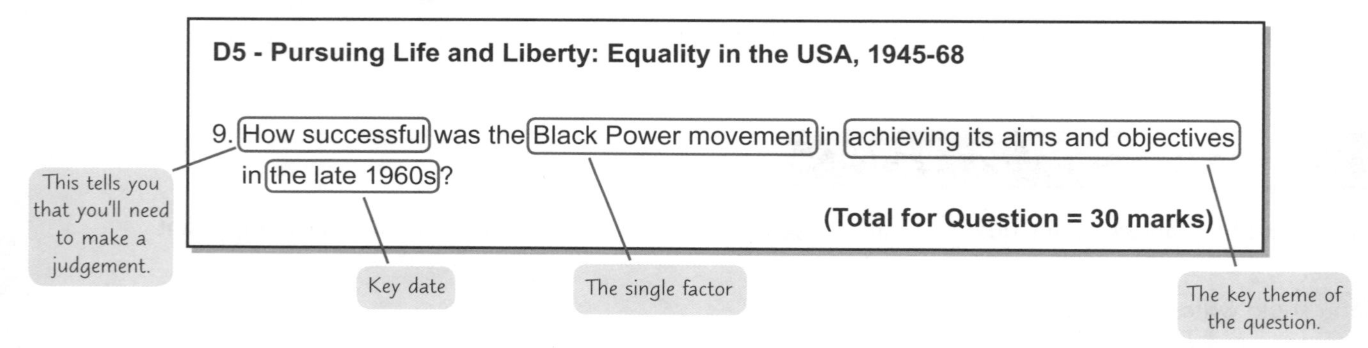
D5 - Pursuing Life and Liberty: Equality in the USA, 1945-68

9. How successful was the Black Power movement in achieving its aims and objectives in the late 1960s?

(Total for Question = 30 marks)

Pick out the **important bits** of the question so you can work out what it's asking you to do:

1) **The judgement** — e.g. 'How successful'. The question is asking you to make a **judgement** as to how successful the **Black Power movement** was in the **late 1960s**.
2) **The single factor** — e.g. 'Black Power movement'. This is the **only** factor you need to **consider**.
3) **The key theme** — e.g. 'achieving its aims and objectives'. The **focus** of your answer will be on the extent to which the **single factor**, Black Power, **achieved success**.
4) **The time period** — e.g. 'the late 1960s'. You should look at the period from **1966**, when **Stokely Carmichael** introduced the **slogan 'Black Power'**, until the **end** of the **decade**. You can **mention** things from **before** and **after** this **time period**, but **don't** go into **too much detail**.

The Examiner wants you to...

1) **Identify** and **explain** the **aims** and **objectives** of the **Black Power movement**.
2) **Consider** how **successful** the **supporters** of **Black Power** were in **achieving** their **aims** and **objectives**.
3) Make a **judgement** as to the **extent** of their success throughout the **late 1960s**.

How to Select the Right Information

Here's another set of lovely pages to show you how to select the relevant information from this book for the exam.

Select the *Information* that's *Relevant* to the *Question*

You need to think about what the **aims** and **objectives** of the **Black Power movement** were.

*You'll find this info on **Page 30**...*

You should mention that the origins of Black Power lay in SNCC and CORE's desire to improve the economic and social status of African Americans.

You could say that Black Power developed because its leaders believed direct action hadn't achieved enough.

This shows the ambiguity surrounding the concept of Black Power.

1) The **Black Power** movement began when **SNCC** and **CORE** developed a more **radical strategy**. They felt the **improvements** in the **legal status** of **African Americans** achieved by **1965** weren't enough, and that there needed to be **major changes** in America's **economy** and **society**. '**Black Power**' became the **slogan** for those who wanted **bigger changes** at a **quicker pace**.
2) **SNCC** and **CORE** underwent a **change of leadership** to reflect this **new ideology**. In **1966 Floyd McKissick** was **elected** as the **head** of **CORE** and **Stokely Carmichael** became **SNCC's chairman**.
3) **McKissick** and **Carmichael** were determined to go in a **radical new direction** — **SNCC** and **CORE** adopted **Malcolm X's** ideas on **black nationalism**, **black separatism** and **self-defence**.
4) In **June 1966 Stokely Carmichael** joined the **March Against Fear** through **Mississippi** to encourage **voter registration**. **Carmichael** used **media coverage** of the march to announce a **new SNCC slogan** — '**Black Power**'.
5) Carmichael **didn't define Black Power**, but it **immediately** became **popular**. For many black people, Black Power **symbolised whatever** they wanted it to **symbolise**. Some saw it as a **demand** for **economic** and **political equality**, others as an affirmation of **black nationalism** and **racial pride**.

*... and on **Page 27**...*

2) **Malcolm** was **critical** of **King's philosophy**. King wanted to end racial discrimination **peacefully** and **integrate white** and **black people**. In contrast, **Malcolm agreed** with **Elijah Muhammad's** view that the **races** should be **kept separate**. He also disliked **King's peaceful protests**, because he felt that **African Americans** were entitled to **fight** for their rights against **white racists** and use violence **if necessary**.
3) He also believed that **African Americans** should **control** the **economy** in their **own communities**, and **shouldn't** use **white people's businesses**. By becoming **economically self-sufficient**, African Americans would no longer be **dependent** on **white people**.

You could briefly write about Malcolm X's aims and objectives, because they influenced the aims of Black Power.

*... and on **Page 31**...*

You could use this to show the ambiguity surrounding the aims and objectives of Black Power.

2) King was **worried** by **Black Power**, which he called a **"slogan without a programme"** — he **didn't** want African Americans to turn to **hatred** and **violence**. **Roy Wilkins**, the **head** of the **NAACP**, believed that **Black Power** was **racism** in **another form**, **no better** than the **racism** of **white supremacists**. The result of this was that **SNCC lost most** of its **funding** and its **ability** to **function** as an **effective** civil rights organisation. SNCC tried to **ally** with the **Black Panthers**, but it **didn't last**.

*... and on **Page 32***

3) The Panthers created a **Ten-Point Programme**, which covered a **wide range** of **issues** that they wanted solving. The first point, which was **influenced** by **Black Power**, called for African Americans to have the **power** and **freedom** to **determine** their **futures**. Moreover, the Panthers wanted **black history** and **black culture** to be **taught** in **schools**.
4) **Several points** referred to **improving** the **economic** and **social inequalities** that **African Americans faced**. For example, the Panthers called for **free health care**, **full employment**, **decent housing** and **education** (which taught the **history** of **African Americans**), as well as **financial compensation** for **centuries** of **slavery** and **oppression**.
5) The Panthers also wanted an **end** to **police brutality**, and for **African Americans** in **prison** to be **released**. They argued that African Americans accused of **crimes** should be **tried** in front of a **jury** of **fellow African Americans**.

You could mention how the Black Panthers, a black power group, laid out their aims. Some of their aims were similar to SNCC's — improvements in the economic and social status of African Americans.

You could state that many of the Panthers' aims and objectives were completely unrealistic.

How to Select the Right Information

Look at the **Achievements** of the **Black Power Movement**

To **judge** how **successful** the **Black Power movement** was, you need to look at some of its **achievements**.

You'll find this info on **Page 30**...

1) **SNCC expelled** its white members in **1966**, which marked a **radical change** in their **ideology**. Some SNCC leaders believed that **African Americans** should **determine** their **own destiny** and that the presence of **senior white members** in **SNCC** led to a feeling of **white superiority**.

You could argue that this was a success because Black Power activists wanted African Americans to take control of the civil rights campaign.

... and on **Page 31**...

You should write about how Black Power succeeded in its aim of giving African Americans a sense of racial pride and self-confidence.

This is a good example of an achievement of the Black Power movement.

1) Black Power led to an increasing emphasis on the study of **black history** and **culture**. African Americans began to embrace their **African heritage** and some even adopted **African names** — for example, **Carmichael** changed his name to **Kwame Toure**. Others sported **Afro hairstyles** to **draw attention** to their **cultural identity**.
2) Black Power had a **positive psychological** effect on African Americans, giving them **greater self-respect** and **pride**. The terms **'Negro'** and **'colored'** fell **out** of **fashion**, and due to the **popularity** of **Black Power**, **African Americans** started to **refer** to **themselves** as **'black'**.
3) Carmichael believed that **Black Power** required **African Americans** to **control** the **communities** they lived in. In **1965**, **Marion Barry**, the **head** of **SNCC** in **Washington, D.C.**, organised the **'Free D.C. Movement'**. Washington, as the national capital, was **controlled directly** by **Congress**. Barry **campaigned successfully** to give the city, which was **majority African American**, **more say** in its **own affairs**. **Barry** later became **mayor** of **Washington, D.C.**

Although it's not a direct link — Black Power helped to change the popular perception of African Americans, an effect which can be seen in TV and films.

2) **African Americans** on **television** and in films were **less likely** to be portrayed as **slow-witted** and **subservient**, instead they were given **leading roles** and their characters were often **professional** and **intelligent**. For example, **Sidney Poitier** played a **detective** in the film ***In the Heat of the Night*** (**1967**) and **Bill Cosby** starred as an undercover **CIA agent** in the TV series ***I Spy*** between **1965** and **1968**. Cosby was given his **own show** in **1969** — ***The Bill Cosby Show***.
3) In **1968** the **musician James Brown** released the single ***Say it Loud — I'm Black and I'm Proud***, after the **assassination** of **Martin Luther King**. Brown's song became an anthem for **African American empowerment**.

... and on **Page 32**...

These are excellent examples to use which show how the Black Panthers were successful in achieving some of their aims and objectives.

It's worth mentioning that the Black Panthers were successful in achieving some aims which were similar to the aims of the mainstream civil rights movement.

1) The **Panthers operated** a **'Patrol the Pigs'** programme, where Panthers **patrolled ghettos** in order to **deter police harassment**, especially of **young African Americans**. **Huey Newton** and other Panthers often **questioned** the **police** to see if they were **abusing** their **power**, but these confrontations sometimes led to **violent clashes**.
2) The **Panthers** created **'survival programmes'**, which were **very popular**, such as the **Free Breakfast programme** which provided **meals** for **thousands** of children in the **ghettos**. The Panthers believed that a **breakfast** would help children **study better** at **school**.
3) **Free health clinics** set up by the Panthers carried out **testing** for **sickle cell anaemia** — a condition which affects many **African Americans**. The Panthers also ran **drug** and **alcohol awareness programmes**.
4) The Panthers set up **'liberation schools'**, which were run by **volunteers**. They taught **black history** and the **achievements** of **black people**. The schools aimed to **promote racial pride** and **self-confidence**.
5) The Panthers also organised **voter registration drives** to get **African Americans** in the **ghettos** to **vote**.

... and on **Page 33**

1) The **head** of the **FBI**, **J. Edgar Hoover**, stated in **1969** that the **Panthers** were the **"greatest threat to the internal security of the country"**. He was **determined** to **destroy them**.

This shows that the Black Panthers succeeded in getting their confrontational and revolutionary image taken seriously.

1) The **notoriety** of the **Panthers** meant that people **took notice** of them, and their **ideology** of **black nationalism** strongly **appealed** to many **African Americans**. For example, **support** for the Panthers among **black soldiers** in **Vietnam** was **widespread**.
2) The Panthers helped many **young black people** to develop a sense of **identity**, and the Panthers were regarded by some as the **embodiment** of **Black Power**.
3) The Panthers ultimately **rejected black nationalism**, condemning it as **black racism**. They believed that they should **lead** a **revolution** of **all races**.

You could mention that the Panthers were successful in getting their ideas across to a lot of African Americans, helping to give them a sense of racial pride and identity.

How to Select the Right Information

Look at the points where **Black Power Didn't Succeed**

To **balance** your essay, you'll need to give examples of the **failures** of the **Black Power movement**.

You'll find this info on **Page 31**...

You could mention that the uncertainty about what Black Power meant led it to be defined by its critics as a solely violent movement. This meant that it never gained the support it needed to achieve its aims.

You could argue that the collapse of SNCC meant that it failed to achieve its aims and objectives.

1) After **SNCC expelled** its **white members** and proclaimed the slogan **'Black Power'**, it scared off **any support** SNCC had from **moderate African Americans** and **white people**. Because Carmichael **never clearly defined** what he meant by **Black Power**, **critics** labelled it a call for **violence**.
2) King was **worried** by **Black Power**, which he called a **"slogan without a programme"** — **he didn't** want African Americans to turn to **hatred** and **violence**. **Roy Wilkins**, the **head** of the **NAACP**, believed that **Black Power** was **racism** in **another form**, **no better** than the **racism** of **white supremacists**. The result of this was that **SNCC lost most** of its **funding** and its **ability** to **function** as an **effective** civil rights organisation. SNCC tried to **ally** with the **Black Panthers**, but it **didn't last**.
3) SNCC's **unrealistic aim** of **black separatism** and its **increasing support** of **violence** caused many people to **distance themselves** from it. SNCC **faded** into **insignificance** and **dissolved altogether** in the **1970s**.

... and on **Page 33**...

3) The Panthers also **split internally**. In **1968**, **Huey Newton** and **Eldridge Cleaver**, a **senior member** of the **Black Panther Party**, argued over the **Panthers' tactics**. **Newton** wanted the Panthers to **focus** on the **survival programmes**, whereas **Cleaver** wanted the Panthers to use **more violence**.
4) By **1970**, after **several gunfights** with the **police**, **internal conflict** and the **unconstitutional harassment** conducted by the **FBI**, many of the **main** Panther **leaders** had been **arrested** or **killed**. The Black Panthers **faded away** in the **1970s** and **dissolved** in **1982**.

Despite the **good work** performed by the **Panthers**, **some** of its **leading members** were **convicted** of **murder** and other **criminal activity**. The Panthers **murdered** one of their **own members** whom they **suspected** of being an **FBI informant**.

You could point out that attempts to unify African Americans and create a long-lasting organisation failed.

... and on **Page 25**

The fact that these problems remained in 1968 shows that the Black Power movement hadn't succeeded in ending discrimination in the US.

1) The **1965 Voting Rights Act** led to a **large increase** in the number of **black voters**.
2) The **majority** of **black children** in the **South** still went to **segregated schools** in **1968**, but the numbers were **declining**. **African Americans** had more chance of going **university** in **1968** than **ever before**.
3) The **segregation** of **facilities**, **buses** and **public places** was coming to an **end**. In some cases **local authorities closed facilities** to **avoid desegregation**, but **hundreds** of **Southern cities** were **desegregated** by **1968**.
4) However, African Americans were still **economically disadvantaged**. Most **African Americans** still worked in **low-skilled** and **low-paid jobs**. In the North, many African Americans lived in **ghettos** (see p.28) — this created **de facto segregation** in other areas such as **education**.
5) The US remained a **divided nation** — in 1968 the **pro-segregationist George Wallace** ran for president as an **American Independent**. In **five states** in the **South** he won **more votes** than the **Democrats** or the **Republicans**.

How to Plan Your Answer

This page will help you plan for a single-factor type question, like the one on page 52.

Use a **Plan** to **Structure** your **Argument**

Here's the question again:

How successful was the Black Power movement in achieving its aims and objectives in the late 1960s?

You have to find a way of **sorting** all the **evidence** into an answer that makes a **judgement**.
You've not got long, so keep your plan **brief**. Here are some things it could include:

1) **1-2 points** on the **aims** and **objectives** of the **Black Power movement**.
2) **2-3 points** on the **successes** of the **Black Power movement**.
3) **2-3 points** on the **failures** of the **Black Power movement**.
4) Some notes on your **conclusion**.

Then you can:

1) Identify any **links** between the points you've thought of.
2) Select **relevant supporting material** for each of your points.
3) Decide **how far** you think Black Power **was successful** in achieving its aims and objectives.

Here's an **Example Plan**

Your plan probably won't be as big as this — we've written it out in full and included a few more points than you'll use in your essays.

Success of the Black Power movement

1. Aims and objectives of the Black Power movement
- There are different interpretations of Black Power, so there are many different aims — lack of focus made it difficult to achieve aims.
- Shared aims — greater economic independence for African Americans, control over black communities, self-confidence, racial pride.
- More radical aims — Ten Point Programme, black separatism, violent revolution etc.

2. Successes of the Black Power movement
- Marion Barry's 'Free D.C. Movement'.
- Racial pride, and pride in African heritage e.g. popularising afro hairstyles.
- Panthers' 'survival programmes'.
- African Americans more assertive and confident — positive portrayal in the media.
- Notoriety of Black Panthers — brought attention to their cause.
- SNCC's expulsion of white members — African Americans controlling civil rights campaign.

3. Failures of Black Power movement
- Failure to define movement. Meant it lacked unity and was perceived as violent.
- Many of the movement's aims were too radical or too unrealistic to achieve.
- SNCC and Panthers collapsed — couldn't unify African Americans, so couldn't achieve their aims and objectives.
- Discrimination still a major problem in 1968 — Black Power had failed to solve major problems.

4. Conclusion
- The Black Power movement succeeded in some of its aims — e.g. the 'Free D.C. movement' and the Panthers' 'survival programmes' helped African Americans to help their communities.
- However, Black Power failed because it didn't achieve many of its aims and objectives, some of which were unrealistic, and African Americans continued to face social and economic discrimination.

Worked Answer

These pages will take an ordinary, everyday, uninspiring answer and turn it into pure exam gold. Ooooooh shiny...

Use your Introduction to get the examiner's Attention

These pages are all about how to word your sentences to impress the examiner, so we haven't included everything from the plan on page 56.

You could write something like this...

Giving specific names and dates shows that you know your stuff.

In June 1966, Stokely Carmichael announced a new slogan, 'Black Power', to describe SNCC's new aims and objectives. Black Power became very important in the late 1960s, but it failed in its main aims and objectives.

This intro is okay because it...
1) **describes** the **importance** of **Black Power**.
2) **names** some of the **key individuals** and **organisations** involved.
3) gives a **brief judgement** by suggesting Black Power **wasn't very successful**.

You could **improve** your introduction by giving some idea of the kind of **successes** and **failures** you're going to **discuss**.

In 1966 the leader of SNCC, Stokely Carmichael, announced the slogan 'Black Power'. Carmichael urged African Americans to use Black Power to fight for equality in the US and make real changes for themselves and their communities. Black Power groups, such as the Black Panthers, went further by calling on African Americans to use violence to fight for their rights. By the late 1960s, the Black Power movement had carried out some community programmes and promoted black culture, but it struggled to achieve much nationally and its radical policies cost them the support of many African Americans.

Here you're showing the examiner some of the points you're going to make in your essay.

This paragraph is more **balanced**, as it shows how **Black Power** was both **successful** and **unsuccessful**.

You could start by Defining the Aims and Objectives of Black Power

You might start your next paragraph with:

Black Power didn't have one single definition, so it's important that you show the examiner that it was interpreted in different ways.

You're showing here that some of the aims of the Black Power movement were unrealistic and therefore unlikely to succeed.

Black Power meant different things to different people. Carmichael believed that Black Power was about African Americans taking control of their communities and asserting their rights. The Black Panther Party aimed to improve the self-esteem and confidence of African Americans, and to lead a violent revolution that would reform US society. Other black power activists supported Malcolm X's views and the unrealistic aim of black nationalism, where African Americans would remove themselves from US society and form their own state.

1) This paragraph is **good** because it introduces the idea that **Black Power** had several **different interpretations** and provides some **examples** of these interpretations.
2) However, you need to **link** this to the **question**. You could add...

Consequently, the Black Power movement couldn't achieve its main aims because it wasn't united. The movement failed to find a leader who could unify African Americans and get them to work together.

Here you're suggesting that because Black Power didn't have a single definition and set of aims it meant that it was less successful.

Worked Answer

Look at the Successes of Black Power

You might start your next paragraph with:

It's good to give people's names if you can remember them.

Black Power organisations successfully enacted some community campaigns. For example Marion Barry led a SNCC campaign to give the black community of Washington, D.C., a greater say in the running of the city. In another community-level scheme, the Black Panthers set up 'survival programmes' which included a Free Breakfast programme and the creation of free health clinics.

1) This paragraph **describes** some of the **successful programmes** carried out by movements **inspired** by **Black Power**, but it **doesn't** link them to the **aims** and **objectives** of **Black Power**.
2) To **improve** this you should link this point to the question — explain **how** these **campaigns furthered** the **aims** and **objectives** of **Black Power**.

One of the main aims of the Black Power movement was for African Americans to take charge of and improve the communities in which they lived. Marion Barry of SNCC led a successful campaign to provide the majority black community of Washington, D.C., with a greater say in the running of their city. The Black Panthers set up 'survival programmes' which included a Free Breakfast programme and the creation of free health clinics. The Panthers' programmes helped poor African Americans and improved life in black communities. Therefore, Barry and the Black Panthers were successful in helping African Americans have more say in the running of their communities, and in improving them, which were key aims and objectives of Black Power.

This links this point back to the question.

Here you've looked at whether these campaigns helped to achieve the aims of Black Power.

Consider how Black Power Wasn't Successful

You could start with:

This clearly signals to the examiner that you're going to develop your argument by looking at how Black Power was less successful.

The Black Power movement failed in many of its aims and objectives. Some of the aims of the Black Power movement were far too unrealistic and radical to ever be achieved.

This is **okay** because you've stated that the **Black Panthers failed** to **achieve** some of its **aims**, but you need to consider **how** these aims were **unsuccessful**.

Try to include details like this to show the examiner that you know the topic.

The Black Power movement was unable to achieve some of its aims and objectives. The Black Panther Party's Ten-Point programme included radical demands for African Americans to be paid financial compensation for centuries of slavery, and for African Americans in prison to be freed. The Panthers were unable to achieve these aims because they weren't realistic.

This is **better** because it gives some examples of the more **radical aims** that the Black Power organisations wanted to achieve, and explains that they had **little chance of success**.

Worked Answer

You should try to **Balance** any points you make

You could write:

> The Black Power movement hoped to unify African Americans to work together to improve their rights. However, the movement failed to attract widespread support, for example the Black Panthers never had more than 10 000 members.

The examiner will be impressed if you use facts and figures like this in your essay.

This is **good** because you've shown that **Black Power groups**, such as the **Black Panthers**, **failed** to **attract** much **support**. However, you can **balance** to this point by **adding**...

> Although the Black Panthers' membership was small, the organisation was popular among young African Americans and black soldiers in Vietnam. The radical demands of the Black Panthers weren't practical, but they gave many African Americans the confidence to stand up and fight for their rights. The Black Power movement also made African Americans proud of who they were, and many embraced their African heritage by choosing African names for themselves or by growing Afros. It could therefore be argued that the Black Power movement achieved its aim of bringing a sense of pride and self-confidence to African Americans.

Here you're showing how some failures and successes were linked. This level of analysis will impress the examiner.

By **balancing** your points you're showing the examiner a **high level** of **analysis**.

Consider both sides of the **Argument** in your **Conclusion**

You could start with...

> On the surface, Black Power wasn't very successful at all. Many of the aims of the Black Power movement weren't realised, such as the aim of black separatism, or of a revolution which would transform US society. Black Power failed in most of its more radical aims because they were too unrealistic to ever be achieved. In the late 1960s African Americans still faced economic and social discrimination — Black Power had not solved these problems.

This links your summary to the question and provides a judgement.

This is **okay**, but you can then **create balance** by **adding** this:

> However, at a local level, some of the objectives of Black Power were achieved. The community campaigns and survival programmes organised by SNCC and the Black Panthers respectively helped African Americans take some control of their communities and improved the lives of African Americans. The Black Power movement was also successful in giving many African Americans a sense of racial pride. African Americans became more confident and self-assured and this influenced black music and the portrayal of black people on television. However, despite these achievements Black Power must be considered a failure because it didn't achieve any of its major revolutionary aims and objectives.

Providing balance like this shows a high level of analysis.

Here you've provided a final judgement.

When you **combine** these **two paragraphs** you create a **balanced conclusion** which shows that the **Black Power movement** had **some successes**, but that its more **radical aims** and **objectives** were **not achieved**.

Sample 'Why' Type Question

The 'why' type of question is the least common type of question you'll come across in the exam, but it's still important that you know how to answer them. So, here's a bunch of pages that tell you all you need to know.

'Why' questions are about Causation

'Why' questions ask you to:

1) **Explain** the reasons a **historical event** or **situation** occurred in the way that it did.
2) Make a **judgement** as to the most **important** causes of the historical event or situation.

Occasionally you'll be asked to consider **two events**, e.g. 'Why was X successful in Y, but not in Z?'

Highlight the Key Words *in the question*

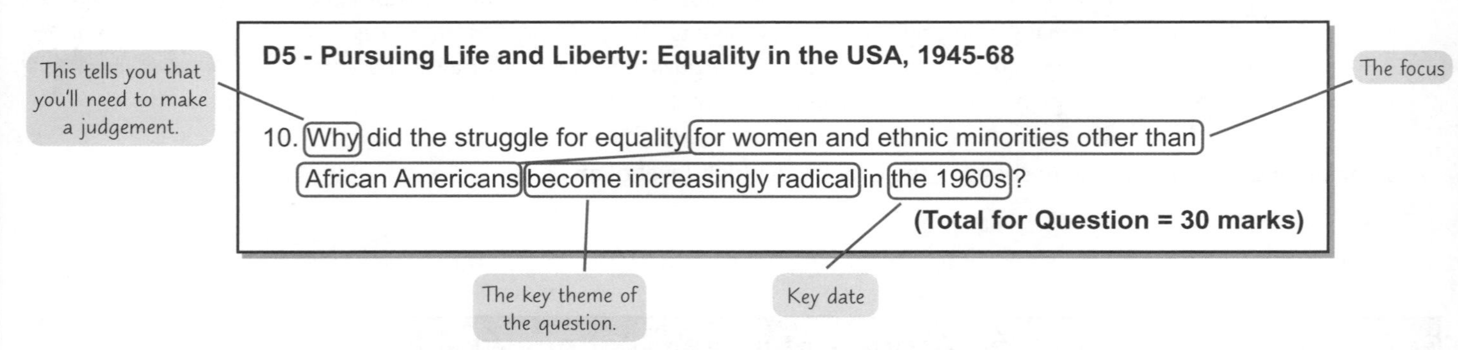

Pick out the **important bits** of the question so you can work out what it's asking you to do:

1) **The key theme** — e.g. 'become increasingly radical'. The question is asking you to make a **judgement** on **why** these groups became **increasingly radical** over time.
2) **The judgement** — e.g. 'Why'. This tells you that you'll have to pick out **key reasons** and decide which is the **most important**.
3) **The focus** — e.g. 'for women and ethnic minorities other than African Americans'. The focus of your answer will be on **women** and the **ethnic minorities** you've **studied** (e.g. **Hispanic** and **Native Americans**).
4) **The time period** — e.g. 'the 1960s'. The question refers to the decade of the **1960s**. You could look at **some things** that happened **before** and **after** this decade, but **don't** go into too much detail.

'Why' questions can be **quite difficult** because they **don't** give you a **factor** in the **question** as a starting point. You have to think of **every point** that should go into your answer yourself.

The Examiner *wants you to...*

1) **Identify** the **methods** used by **women** and **ethnic minorities** in their struggle for equality, and the ways in which thettse **methods changed** during the **1960s**.

2) **Suggest reasons** why these methods became **increasingly radical** over time.

3) Make a **judgement** on **which reason** you think was the **most** important in **explaining why** women and ethnic minorities became **increasingly radical** in the **1960s**.

How to Select the Right Information

Here's the last set of mind-blowing pages which show you how to select the relevant information for the exam.

Select the Information that's Relevant to the Question

The question is asking you **why** the struggle for equality for **women** and **various ethnic minorities** became **increasingly radical** in the **1960s**, so it's worth looking at the **context** in which **women's** and **ethnic minority groups** were **operating**.

*You'll find this info on **Page 35**...*

4) After the Second World War there was a **baby boom** in the US, which meant that by the **1960s** there was a **large population** of **teenagers**. These young Americans were more **politically aware** than their parents' generation. This was because they'd received a **good education** and because of the **increasing availability** of **television**, which enabled them to **witness** the **prejudice** displayed **against African Americans**, and some of the horrors of the **Vietnam War**.

> You could mention the fact that the youth of the 1960s were very politically active and aware of the prejudices in their society.

The **privileged economic position** of many young Americans meant that they **didn't** have to get **jobs** straight after school, and could go to **university**. This gave them the ability to become **involved** in **campaigns**.

> This shows that young people were more able to become involved in campaigns.

1) In **1960**, **students** in **Michigan** formed the **Students for a Democratic Society** (**SDS**), an **organisation** that campaigned for **economic equality**. The **SDS** were part of a **growing movement** in the **1960s** known as the **'New Left'** — a term used to describe **organisations** led by **young radicals** who wanted a more **equal society** in the **US**.
2) The **SDS** led high-profile campaigns **against** the **Vietnam War**.

> This shows that radicalism was developing in the 1960s.

- In **March 1965 President Johnson escalated** the **US's involvement** in **Vietnam**, sending **thousands** of **young American men** to **fight** the **communists**.
- In **April 1965**, the SDS led an anti-war protest of around **20 000** people in **Washington, D.C.**
- The SDS were also involved with several other **anti-war protests** including **teach-ins** where teachers and students debated the war rather than having lessons.
- **Students** formed a strong opposition to the war — many **feared** being **conscripted** into the army to fight in Vietnam. Some civil rights groups such as **SNCC** and **CORE** opposed the war too.
- The **Vietnam War** led to the **deaths** of **millions** of people — the US used **hugely destructive bombing** against the **North Vietnamese**, and sprayed **toxic defoliants** on the **jungle**. This made many young Americans **question** their **government's morality** and whether the **US** really was a **force for good**.

> You could mention that the Vietnam War saw the growth of a protest culture led by radical groups like the SDS.

3) **Young Americans**, particularly those who went to college, also got involved with the **civil rights movement**, **women's liberation** organisations (see p.39) and **environmental** organisations such as **Friends of the Earth** (formed in **1969**).

> This shows that the protest culture led to young Americans joining campaigns on issues such as women's liberation.

1) Some young Americans **rejected** the **conformity** of **American society**, which **expected** people to **act** in a **certain way** (e.g. get jobs, get married, raise children). These people formed the **counterculture movement**.
2) The **counterculture movement** included groups like **hippies** (young people who didn't want to conform to what mainstream society expected), **anti-war campaigners** (such as the SDS) and **feminists** (campaigners for women's rights). They had different beliefs and aims, but they all **challenged** the **social** and **cultural norms** of **1960s America**.
3) **Music** was an important part of the counterculture. **Criticism** of the **Vietnam War** and of **US society** was common in **1960s music**. **Bob Dylan's** song ***The Times They Are A-Changin'*** summed up the feeling that there was a **youth-led rebellion** which would **create** a **different society**.
4) A **drugs** culture developed in the **1960s**. The **psychedelic music** of artists like **Jimi Hendrix** was influenced by the **hallucinogenic** drug **LSD**.

> You could mention that campaigners in the 1960s didn't accept society as it was — they rebelled against social and cultural norms and injustices.

> You could argue that young people in the 1960s felt that their parents' generation had failed to create a fair society, and that new tactics were needed to tackle injustice.

How to Select the Right Information

Look at the **Problems Hispanic** and **Native Americans Faced**

You should look at the **issues** that **Hispanic** and **Native Americans** were dealing with in this period and why this led them to use **increasingly radical methods** to secure better rights for themselves.

*You'll find this info on **Page 36...***

1) From the **early 1950s**, **Hispanic Americans** began to organise themselves to demand **better working** and **living conditions**, and to secure **basic civil rights**. In **1951** the **American Council of Spanish-speaking People** (**ACSSP**) was formed to **combat discrimination** in areas such as **housing**, **employment** and **education**.
2) **After** the **Brown v Board of Education** ruling (see pages 12-13), the **ACSSP** and the **NAACP** occasionally worked together to **desegregate schools**.
3) **Cesar Chavez** campaigned for the **rights** of **farm workers**, many of whom were **Hispanic**. The farm workers were **very poorly paid** and had **few labour rights**. From **1952** he began to organise **voter registration drives** and campaigned against **racial discrimination** towards **Hispanic Americans**.
4) In **1962 Chavez** formed the **National Farm Workers Association** (**NFWA**), which later became **United Farm Workers** (**UFW**) — the first farm union in the US. The **NFWA** used non-violent direct action, such as **boycotts**, **peaceful protests** and **pickets** (peaceful crowds that act as a barrier), to campaign for **improved rights** for **farm workers**. In **1965** it began a **prolonged strike**, which secured **higher wages** for **workers** on large **commercial grape farms**.

These are some examples you can use of problems that Hispanic Americans faced.

You should mention that Chavez used non-violent direct action to campaign for better rights.

1) Some Hispanic Americans formed **radical organisations** like the **Young Chicanos for Community Action** (**YCCA**). The **YCCA** evolved into the **Brown Berets**, who had **similar tactics** to the **Black Panthers** (see pages 32-33).
2) The Brown Berets wore **army-style uniforms** and **monitored** the **police** to make sure they didn't harass Hispanic Americans. They also worked on **community programmes** to **improve housing**, **education**, **employment** and **health care**, and **protested against** the **Vietnam War**.
3) In **March 1968** the **Brown Berets** organised a series of '**school dropouts**', known as the '**Chicano Blowouts**', in which Hispanic American students **left** their **classes** to **protest against** the **poor standard** of their **education**.
4) The Brown Berets suffered from a **lack** of **clear aims**, **police harassment** and **in-fighting**. They **dissolved** in **1972**.
5) In the **late 1960s**, young Hispanic Americans from **Puerto Rico** formed the **Young Lords**. The **Young Lords** were **similar** to the **Black Panthers** — they organised **community campaigns** and tried to stop **police harassment** of Hispanic Americans. They also campaigned for **women's equality**.

- However, the **rise** of **radicalism** among **Hispanic Americans** shows that many were still **frustrated** by the **economic** and **social status** of **Hispanic Americans**. Despite **voter registration drives**, Hispanic Americans were **under-represented** among American voters, which meant they had **little political power**.

This shows that radical groups, such as the Brown Berets, formed to fight for equality.

This tells you what issues a radical Hispanic organisation campaigned about.

You could mention that education was another problem issue for Hispanic Americans.

You could argue that poor social and economic conditions would have led to frustration and a willingness to try more radical tactics.

*... and on **Page 37***

1) **Termination** was introduced to tackle **poverty** among Native Americans. The **government pushed individual tribes** to **agree** to **give up** their **legal existence** so that **Native Americans** would be like **any other US citizens**.
2) The government offered to **buy reservations** and **redistribute** the **money** to Native Americans. The government also **helped Native Americans integrate** into **US society** — a **relocation programme** was **offered** which included **financial incentives** to **encourage** them to **move** to **towns** and **cities**.
3) However, like African Americans, the **Native Americans** experienced **discrimination** and **hardship** in the **cities**. Many Native Americans **struggled** to **adjust** to **urban life**, and **suffered** due to **unemployment** and **alcoholism**.
4) Many Native Americans felt that **termination threatened** their **cultural identity**, and so the **NCAI** campaigned **against** it. In 1970 **President Richard Nixon ended** the **termination policy**.

You could argue that urban poverty led to radicalism, as it had for African Americans.

You could mention that threats to their culture worried many Native Americans.

1) In **1961** the **National Indian Youth Council** (**NIYC**) was established. NIYC was **more radical** than the **NCAI** and, following the example of the civil rights movement, decided that **direct action** was **more** likely to be **successful** than the **NCAI's legal tactics**. For example, NIYC organised '**fish-ins**' as a way of **asserting** their **right** to **fish** in several rivers.
2) In **1968** the **American Indian Movement** (**AIM**) was founded. It adopted the same **aggressive approach** used by the **Black Panthers** (see pages 32-33), and used the slogan '**Red Power**'. Inspired by the **Panthers**, **AIM patrolled neighbourhoods** wearing **red jackets** and **berets**, and **monitored police harassment** of **Native Americans**.
3) In **1969** a group called the **Indians of All Tribes** (**IAT**) occupied the disused prison on **Alcatraz Island** in **California**. They claimed the **island belonged** to **Native Americans**, not the US government. The remaining protesters were **removed** in **1971** by **US government officers**.

Between **1945** and **1968**, **Native Americans** made **some progress** in **challenging racial discrimination**, but many **Native Americans** still faced a great deal of **poverty**. However, despite the policy of **termination**, **Native Americans** still maintained their **separate languages** and **cultural identities**.

Use this to give examples of groups that used more radical methods, the methods they used and examples of the issues that led to this radicalism.

You could argue that the threats to their different cultures and languages drove many Native Americans to more radical methods.

How to Select the Right Information

Look at the **Problems Women Faced**

Finally, you need to look at **issues** which were **affecting women** in this period and **why** they became **increasingly radical** in order to **achieve equal rights**.

You'll find this info on **Page 38**...

You could mention that unhappiness among women led them to question their role in society and campaign for change.

4) One **result** of **early marriage** was that many **young women** didn't **graduate** from **university**. In **1960**, only **37%** of **women** who attended university actually **graduated** — many who **dropped out** did so in order to **marry**.
5) **However**, by the **end** of the **1950s** many women were **unhappy** with their **low status** in **society**, and with the **dull everyday routine** of being housewives and mothers. **Doctors reported** that many **housewives slept** for up to **ten hours** a **day**, and **millions** were **taking tranquillizers** to relieve their **unhappiness** and **boredom**.

1) Those women who did **work for a living** were **paid less** than their **male colleagues**. **Women** were usually **confined** to **certain professions**, such as **secretarial work**, **nursing**, **waitressing** and **teaching**.
2) In **1961 President Kennedy** established a **Commission on the Status of Women**, chaired by **President Roosevelt's widow**, **Eleanor**. The **Commission reported** that there was **widespread discrimination** against women:
   - **Women didn't** receive **equal pay** to men for **equal work**.
   - **Employers** often **refused** to **hire women**.
   - **In 1960** only **7%** of **doctors** and **around 4%** of **lawyers** were **women**.
3) Things did **improve** for **women** — in **1963 Kennedy passed** the **Equal Pay Act**, which **guaranteed equal pay** for **men** and **women** who **performed** the **same duties**, while the **1964 Civil Rights Act outlawed discrimination** against women in the field of **employment**.
4) However, these **laws** were **often ignored** in practice, so women began to set up their own **women's liberation groups** to **campaign** for real **change**.

These are examples you could use of problems that women faced.

You should mention that these problems caused frustration and resentment among women.

You could argue that a lack of real changes following changes in the law encouraged more radical action — as can be seen from the turn to direct action by black organisations following the NAACP's successes.

... and on **Page 39**

You could write about the role that Friedan played in the struggle for women's rights.

1) In **1963 Betty Friedan** published the **influential book**, ***The Feminine Mystique***. In it she claimed that **women** were **suffering** because they were told by the **media** that they should feel **fulfilled** as **housewives** and **mothers** — women who **didn't** feel fulfilled by this life felt like **failures**.
2) Friedan accused **television**, **women's magazines** and **advertisers** of creating a **false image** of **women**, and called on women to press for **change**. As **more women** got **jobs** they felt **increasingly empowered** to **demand equality**.
3) In **1966 Friedan** set up the **National Organisation for Women** (**NOW**), which was termed **"an NAACP for women"**. **NOW used** many of the **NAACP's techniques**, including **lawsuits** and **boycotts**.

1) More and more women began to **identify themselves** as **feminists** — people who **campaigned** for **equal rights** for women — and they **engaged** in the **political issues** of the era. Women were **influential** in **demonstrations against** the **Vietnam War** and **in favour** of **African-American civil rights**.
2) However, women were often treated unequally in organisations such as **SNCC** and the **SDS** (see p.35), which were often **sexist** and **patronising**. Female activists **complained** that while **American men** showed **empathy** for the **Vietnamese** or **African Americans**, they **showed none** for American **women**.
3) When **SNCC expelled** its **white members** in **1966**, many of its former white female members **joined** either **NOW** or the more **radical feminist organisations**. These women brought with them the **tactics** they'd developed in **direct action** and **community campaigning**.

You could mention that female activists were radicalised by their involvement in anti-Vietnam War and civil rights campaigns.

It's worth saying that the expulsion of female members from SNCC helped to radicalise the women's movement.

More radical methods like this show that feminists were trying to gain attention for their cause.

You could argue that because things were slow to change, women became more frustrated and took a more radical approach to women's liberation.

1) Radical feminists **rejected** what they saw as a **male-dominated society** and the **institutions** of that society, such as **marriage** and **family**. They felt that women should **lead** their **own society**.
2) In **1967**, feminists in **New York** formed the **New York Radical Women** (**NYRW**). In **1968** NYRW organised a **demonstration against** the **Miss America pageant** in **Atlantic City**, **New Jersey**. **NYRW members** crowned a **sheep** as their own **'Miss America'**.
4) However, **ingrained attitudes** towards women, especially views on the **role** of **women** in the **home**, were **slow** to **change**. Many women were **uneasy** about **feminism** and some **opposed** it.

How to Plan Your Answer

This page will help you plan for 'why' type questions, like the one on page 60.

*Use a **Plan** to **Structure** your **Argument***

Here's the question again:

Why did the struggle for equality for women and ethnic minorities other than African Americans become increasingly radical in the 1960s?

Once you've got your **evidence** you have to **organise** it into an essay.
A plan will help you do this. You shouldn't spend more than **5 minutes** on it, so **don't** waste time.
Your plan could include:

1) **1-2 points** on the **protest culture** of the **1960s**.
2) **2-3 points** on the **increasing radicalism** of **ethnic minority groups**.
3) **2-3 points** on the **increasing radicalism** of **women's groups**.
4) **1-2 points** on the **influence** of the **black civil rights movement**.
5) Some notes on your **conclusion**.

Then you can:

1) Select **relevant supporting material** for each point.
2) Identify any **links** between the points you've thought of.
3) **Decide** which factor you think was the **most important**.

Your plan probably won't be as big as this — we've written it out in full and included a few more points than you'll use in your essays.

*Here's an **Example Plan***

Radicalism — ethnic minority and women's groups

1. Protest Culture in the 1960s
- Youth more politically active and involved in civil rights campaigns.
- Protest movements led by radicals, e.g. SDS.
- Youth more willing to challenge older generation and try new, radical tactics.

2. Causes and methods of radicalism — ethnic minorities
- Hispanic Americans faced police harassment and discrimination in housing, employment and education.
- Hispanic Americans' increasing radicalism — Cesar Chavez's non-violent direct action. Militant groups, e.g. Brown Berets and Young Lords, patrolled police, community campaigns, 'Chicano Blowouts'.
- Native Americans faced termination policy, police harassment and problems living in cities, e.g. alcoholism, unemployment.
- Native Americans' increasing radicalism — NIYC's fish-ins. AIM patrolled police. IAT occupied Alcatraz.

3. Causes and methods of radicalism — women
- Women faced — discontentment with life at home, discrimination at work, failure of de jure changes to make de facto changes.
- Women's increasing radicalism — role of Betty Friedan. NOW's campaigns. Growth of groups such as NYRW.

4. Influence of African Americans
- Highest profile ethnic minority group, other groups seemed to follow same pattern — direct action then more radical. Influence of Black Power.
- Black Panthers influenced AIM and Brown Berets — style and activities.
- NOW set up as NAACP for women.
- SNCC's expulsion of white members led to radicalism of women's groups.

5. Conclusion
- Many factors led to increasing radicalism — protest culture and frustration over continuing problems.
- Biggest influence was the Black Power movement — seen in style and tactics of Hispanic and Native American groups. Expulsion helped radicalise women's groups.

Worked Answer

Ahh... we're almost finished, but before I go, here are some more pages that will help you to improve your essays.

*A good **Introduction** will **Guide** your essay*

These pages are all about how to word your sentences to impress the examiner, so we haven't included everything from the plan on page 64.

You could start with:

> There were many reasons why the struggle for equality for women and ethnic minority groups became increasingly radical in the 1960s. Women and ethnic minorities faced a great deal of discrimination and inequality, which created frustration and led to a rise in radicalism. These groups were also influenced by the protest culture in the 1960s, and the increasing radicalism of the black civil rights movement.

You've identified the points that you're going to write about.

This intro is **okay** because it: 1) **Focuses** on the **question**.
2) Briefly mentions that there was some **change over time**.

However, it's a bit **vague**. A **better** introduction would include more **detail**, like this:

> Women, Native Americans and Hispanic Americans began to seek greater equality in the 1960s, and their methods changed over time. These groups initially tried to solve the discrimination and inequality they faced through legal battles, but they became frustrated by their lack of progress and turned to more radical methods. This move toward radicalism was influenced by several factors, including the protest culture in the 1960s, and the increasing radicalism of the black civil rights movement after 1966.

Here you're clearly showing that there was change over time towards more radical methods.

*You could start by looking at the **Protest Culture** in the **1960s***

You could begin with:

> Young people in the 1960s were very politically active and took part in civil rights campaigns and anti-Vietnam War protests because they wanted to rebel against the injustices that they saw in society. The protest culture in the 1960s, led by radical groups such as the Students for a Democratic Society (SDS), was very influential.

This is a good point — but you need to link it to women, Hispanic and Native Americans.

1) These sentences just **describe** the **protest culture** and **increasing radicalism**, especially among **young Americans**, in the **1960s**.
2) To improve this you need to **link** it to the **question**.

> One of the reasons why ethnic minority and women's groups became more radical in this period was that they were influenced by the protest culture of the 1960s. Radical groups, such as the Students for a Democratic Society (SDS), were prepared to challenge authority and take dramatic steps to further their causes, and this influenced women's and ethnic minorties' rights groups. For example, young Native Americans challenged authority by breaking away from older civil rights groups — the more radical National Indian Youth Council (NIYC) took a different approach to campaigning for equality than the more conservative National Council of American Indians (NCAI) — they took direct action instead of legal action.

This clearly links the point to the question.

Worked Answer

You could the look at the **Specific Problems Ethnic Minorities** faced

You could start with:

> Ethnic minorities faced many problems in the 1960s. Hispanic Americans faced discrimination in housing, employment and education, while Native Americans found it difficult to fit into mainstream American life and suffered from alcoholism and unemployment. Both Hispanic and Native Americans had difficulties with the police. These problems caused a great deal of anger among ethnic minorities.

It's good to briefly list examples to show the examiner what you intend to discuss later.

This introduces the idea that **ethnic minorities** faced **many problems**, but it doesn't explain **why** this led them to become **increasingly radical** in the **1960s**.

To **improve** this you could write:

> Ethnic minority groups became more radical in the 1960s because they grew frustrated with the many problems that they faced, such as discrimination in housing, employment and education. Native Americans found it difficult to live in American towns and many suffered from alcoholism and unemployment. Moreover, both Hispanic and Native Americans had to deal with police harassment. African Americans had similar problems and many turned to Black Power as a way of tackling them — they formed militant groups such as the Black Panthers. The Panthers provided an example for the Brown Berets and AIM, who used some of the Panthers' radical methods to address the problems their communities faced — they patrolled the police to monitor harassment and organised community campaigns to improve living conditions.

Linking ethnic minority organisations to the work of the Black Panthers shows you have a broad knowledge of the period.

You should look for **Links** between **Points**

You could start with:

> The Black Power movement led to SNCC's decision to expel white members, as they believed that African Americans should lead their own organisations. Many of the white female activists who were expelled joined feminist organisations.

This paragraph introduces the idea that **Black Power** led to **white female activists** joining **feminist organisations**. However, this could be **linked more clearly** to the **question**. You could write...

> Black Power was an influence on many organisations' radicalism, but it helped to radicalise the women's movement in a different way. When SNCC expelled its white members in 1966, many of the white female activists who were forced to leave went on to join women's rights organisations. They brought with them the tactics and experience that they had developed at SNCC, which contributed to the increasing radicalism of women's rights organisations in the late 1960s.

This clearly links this point to the question.

You need to explain why each point is important.

This is **better** because you've shown how this **point relates** to the **question** and given a **reason** why **SNCC's expulsion** of **white female activists** led to **women's organisations** becoming **increasingly radical**. Make sure that **every point** you make is **linked** to the **question**, otherwise you'll write things that **aren't relevant**.

Worked Answer

Summarise the **Points** you've made in your **Essay**

Your conclusion should **summarise** the **key points** that you've made in each paragraph.
If you've linked your paragraphs well then you'll have **created an argument**.

> Native American, Hispanic American and women's rights organisations became increasingly radical through the 1960s due to a number of factors, including the influence of radical protest groups in the 1960s, frustration over the problems ethnic minorities and women faced, and the influence of the Black Power movement.

This is **okay**, but you need to provide some **detail** to show **why** there was **change over time** towards **radicalism**, because that is what the question is asking for.

> Native American, Hispanic American and women's organisations became increasingly radical through the 1960s due to a number of factors. The protest culture of the 1960s saw a growth in radical groups and this influenced many ethnic minority and female activists to challenge the methods of older civil rights groups and turn to more radical methods. Frustration over the problems that Hispanic and Native Americans faced led to a desire to take more radical action, and they followed the example of Black Power and the Black Panthers by forming militant groups such as the Brown Berets and AIM in the late 1960s. Women's groups also became more radical, as they were frustrated by the lack of real change following the 1963 Equal Pay Act. They recognised that they needed new tactics if they were going to change society as well as the law.

By giving these dates you're showing how these movements became more radical over time.

This paragraph **summarises** the **changes** that **occurred** in the **1960s** and gives reasons as to **why** they occurred.

Finish your conclusion with a **Final Assessment**

Your conclusion should end with a **judgement**. Your judgement should identify which **factor** you think was the **most important** in causing ethnic minority and women's groups' struggle for equality to become **increasingly radical**.

You could try...

> Black Power was the most important factor in the increasing radicalism of ethnic minority and women's organisations.

This shows the examiner that you've made a clear judgement.

This conclusion makes a **judgement**, but it's **not enough** on its own. You can **improve** this with more **detail** and an **explanation** of the choice that you've made:

> Black Power had the biggest influence on the increasing radicalism of ethnic minority and women's groups in the 1960s. Women's and ethnic rights groups followed the example of black civil rights groups by making more radical demands and adopting a more confrontational style.

This provides an explanation for your judgement.

Index

Index

Index